I Talk To Strangers

(upstairs and downstairs)

CAROLE CHANDLER

BALBOA.
PRESS
A DIVISION OF HAY HOUSE

Balboa Press books may be ordered through booksellers or by contacting:

Balboa Press
A Division of Hay House
1663 Liberty Drive
Bloomington, IN 47403
www.balboapress.com
1-(877) 407-4847

Because of the dynamic nature of the Internet, any web addresses or links contained in this book may have changed since publication and may no longer be valid. The views expressed in this work are solely those of the author and do not necessarily reflect the views of the publisher, and the publisher hereby disclaims any responsibility for them.

The author of this book does not dispense medical advice or prescribe the use of any technique as a form of treatment for physical, emotional, or medical problems without the advice of a physician, either directly or indirectly. The intent of the author is only to offer information of a general nature to help you in your quest for emotional and spiritual well-being. In the event you use any of the information in this book for yourself, which is your constitutional right, the author and the publisher assume no responsibility for your actions.

Any people depicted in stock imagery provided by Thinkstock are models, and such images are being used for illustrative purposes only. Certain stock imagery © Thinkstock.

Printed in the United States of America

ISBN: 978-1-4525-6704-4 (sc)
ISBN: 978-1-4525-6706-8 (hc)
ISBN: 978-1-4525-6705-1 (e)

Library of Congress Control Number: 2013900810

Balboa Press rev. date: 1/18/2013

I talk to strangers. Why? They talk to me

Have strangers always talked to me? Not a chance

What changed? Me

Why did I change? Well something had to be done

How did I change? Focus

What was the result? Misery to joy in one lifetime

Can anyone create this change? Yes, anyone

*

Changes took place in every aspect of my existence and I started experiencing a profound difference in the way people responded to me, everywhere I went.

Over time I told a few friends about what someone said here or what another person said there. They enjoyed my tales and suggested I share my experiences. I considered writing a book but hesitated about where, when and how.

I went to Ireland for a few days this year and the result was my first book, *'to be sure to be sure to be sure'*. In retrospect it was simply the warm up. Then my second book was born with tales of interactions *'here, there and everywhere'*.

This is my third. Enjoy.

*

I have been well and truly bitten by the writing bug. When my second book creation had finished taking shape, I thought I needed a break but that idea was soon overridden by my urge to enjoy the momentum. To my surprise this creative force has more power than I had imagined and I find myself launching into my third book, without taking the holiday which I had promised myself. There is some probability that people who enjoy the first two may be inclined to try this one, so as I find my literary juices flowing freely, I may as well stay with this energy and write while my enthusiasm is still strong. Ooh what fun. My tales of strangers talking to me on buses are waiting to be shared and while I have not decided precisely how I will proceed, it will be interesting to see how this publication unfolds.

I am tempted to quote Julie Andrews from one of my favourite feel good movies, *'Let's start at the very beginning, a very good place to start...'* The only problem is that I am unaware of the beginning of my bus adventures. They have evolved so gradually that I did not even notice them happening. I guess there are many reasons why my experiences were so different where I used to live, so interestingly my lovely new interactions have mostly happened during the past few years.

One of my earliest moments when I noticed some kind of difference taking place was when I sat at the bus stop at the top of my road, where I used to live on the Surrey London borders. While waiting for a number 33 to Hammersmith, I noticed the same driver of a 493 which stopped at the same place. He obviously remembered me too because over time he progressed from a nod, to a nod and smile, to a triple combo of nod, smile and wave. I was new to the stranger thing and his acknowledgement of me was a big deal. He probably thought nothing of it but I remember feeling good about receiving his cheery greetings. When I moved to Tooting, I saw him occasionally on the same route by which time I was well accustomed to drivers waving at me and it felt good to see him again.

*

Okay, next I feel like returning to the memory of an encounter a couple of years ago, when I boarded a number 77 from the Wimbledon Road stop on Garratt Lane early one Sunday morning. I had decided to treat myself to a fun time at the South Bank's Royal Festival Hall and was excited to see which genre of free musical treat would be in store for me in the foyer that day. I have previously enjoyed listening to some wonderful choirs and musical accompaniments for dance workshops, when sometimes the only reasonable thing to do is to just let go of all inhibitions and sing along.

So with my keen anticipation for the delights ahead, I boarded the double decker and did what I always do, I smiled and said hallo to the driver. Well of course I did, I mean why wouldn't? After all he was doing me the honour of driving me from home to my destination, so the very least I could do was offer a simple cheerful salutation at no cost and little effort. After a smile, a hallo and a bleep of my trusty Oyster card, I sat upstairs at the front for my travelling enjoyment. I shall say it now and I suspect I may say it again, that sitting upstairs at the front of a double decker bus is the best show in town. Fact.

The route for this service ends in Waterloo, this was my stop anyway and the bus was going no further, so I did what I always do, I walked to the front of the bus to say thank you to the driver. Well of course I did, I mean, why wouldn't? After all he had done me the honour or driving me from home to my destination, so the very least I could do was offer him a few simple cheerful words of gratitude at no cost and little effort.

I do this because I like to say thank you. It makes me feel good and if the driver responds, that is a bonus. Sometimes they do and sometimes they do not, either way it is fine with me. I understand that everyone has 'stuff' going on in their lives so there can be a multitude of reasons why someone may be feeling a tad grumpy. Let's face it, I had chosen to travel into town on a Sunday morning and I appreciate that other people might prefer to do other things with their lives at that time of the day. Who knows, perhaps I would have chosen differently if I had a car to wash in the street, a dog to walk in the park, a partner to cuddle under the duvet, a church to share hymns with others or one of the many other Sunday morning activities which may have been taking place elsewhere.

I said thank you to the driver and I started walking away, what I did not expect was for him to call me back. He wanted to talk to me. Why? Apparently, because I had said thank you and apparently that was unusual. He said that I was unusual for doing it. He had more to say. He also wanted to speak to me because he had noticed me when I boarded. Why? Apparently, because I had said hallo and apparently that was unusual. He said that I was unusual for doing it. He had more to say. In fact he was jolly chatty indeed. We conversed for several minutes there on his otherwise empty bus. He introduced himself and he really liked my name. When he asked me if I was going to church, it was my instinct to say that wherever I am is my church, my spiritual home is wherever I want it to be but I decided to keep those thoughts to myself, as I probably did not know him well enough to embark on that level of discussion. He told me about his recent holiday, said a few things about his darling mother and we parted wishing each other a good day. How nice of this lovely man to so willingly engage me in conversation. How lovely of this nice man to allow me to encroach on his valuable break time between journeys. He could have quite easily let me go when I first spoke to him and locked himself on his passenger free bus to enjoy some quiet time, before the next lot of people joined him. He could have quite easily hidden on his bus and pretended to be invisible, as so many drivers do (bless them) when having a well-earned rest. Yet here was this delightful man giving me access to him and his time by sharing joyful conversation. I am blessed.

A couple of weeks later I was walking along Garratt Lane when I heard the hoot of a horn. I ignored it. I heard it again, I ignored it. I crossed the road, heard the hooting tooting again and ignored it again. Why did I ignore it repeatedly? No particular reason, except that when I am walking, I generally focus my attention on the present moment, finding the beauty in something to observe and ignore distractions which do not concern me such as sirens, car horns, some forms of human activity and such like.

By the time I had crossed the road I became aware of a vehicle driving slowly beside me, not just any vehicle but a double decker bus. I vaguely wondered why it was moving quite so slowly when I heard the tooting hooting again and guessed that it was coming from the slow mover. Perfectly convinced that the noise could have little to do with me, I idly glanced in the direction of the large red people transporter, only to find the driver waving energetically at me. Guess who? It was my chap from the Sunday morning conversation time at Waterloo. What a sweetheart. Not only did he remember me but he went to all that trouble to attract my attention. I mean seriously, what a sweetheart.

I was more than a little bit surprised because he was between stops, with several people on board, who probably wondered what on earth was going on. Oh bless him, he made my day. I have had the pleasure of seeing him since and enjoyed a cheerful greeting or nod or wave from a distance. Once I even saw him standing at a bus stop in Tooting Broadway, where he told me that he was working overtime on what should have been his day off and looking forward to the remainder of the Bank Holiday weekend. He was an absolute darling and all of this was the result of a simple hallo.

*

So here I am already having fun reliving a wonderful meeting-a-driver interaction. There are plenty of driver related stories to share but more about the angels of the road later. I am following the urge to chat about others who are not officially controlling transport but who may equally drive us around the bend or even drive or crazy for one reason or another. However, my aim is to keep my tales in a positive frame of mind. It is possible that I may slip up once or twice, so I apologise in advance if I get carried away. Lots of less than positive stories can be told about what this person said or what that person did, revolving around people being upset about one thing or another. They are so often the stuff of soap operas and my goal here is quite different.

For more clarification about where I am coming from, why I think the way I do and what makes me tick, of course it is not compulsory but this book will make considerably more sense if my previous books have been read. My first book *'I Talk to Strangers – to be sure, to be sure, to be sure'* has turned out to be my warm up. Then in *'I Talk to Strangers – here there and everywhere'* I really got going and gave some extended attention to why, who, how, where and when of my journey, leading to the joyful existence which I experience now. In short, my life has been transformed as a direct result of changing my way of thinking. A major change is that strangers never used to talk to me and they do now. Anyone who is inspired to learn more is welcome to delve into my previous publications, as I envisage this one being primarily devoted to the variety of bus related encounters which have been sent my way.

*

For readers who are used to me and those who are new to me, here is a teeny weeny glimpse of how my mind works.

Today I watched a fly. I watched it for ages as it took the long trek up the window pane upstairs on a number 319 bus from Clapham Junction to Streatham. When I say fly, I could not tell you which type, I suppose there are hundreds, possibly thousands of classifications and sub categories for small winged creatures. I confess to not knowing specifics. This little creature was teeny with a body about two millimetres long and fine translucent wings trailing behind. His legs were like short blond eyelashes and would have been invisible against the light but I observed him closely because I was interested in him, I was interested in how he looked and how he moved and then I wondered why he was here at all.

He looked beautiful. I decided that he was perfectly formed, perfect in every way, not so unlike us. With his lightly coloured body and even lighter wings I struggled to maintain my focus on him, as he continued his long walk, with the bright blue sky in the background. Up, up, up the pane he travelled in a straight line straight up, using his tentacles he seemed to manage really well. Then again I had no idea what his goal was. Did he have an appointment with a similar creature up there in the bus? Was he looking for food up there in the bus? Did he even know that he was up there in the bus?

He moved forward without straying to the left or the right, I wondered how he even knew that he was going straight. Perhaps he did not know, perhaps he did not need to know. He covered some ground in miniscule insect terms, when after some minutes and about thirty centimetres he executed a sudden change of plan. He released his grip on the glass and allowed himself to drop. Why did he not use his wings? Mine is not to question why. He dropped down. Where did he go? I looked below and there he was making another trek of a new course up my thigh. He was much easier to observe as his yellow form contrasted with my black trousers. I watched him walk upwards then offered him the index finger of my left hand, by way of providing interest of a previously undiscovered terrain. He accepted the offer immediately.

Mr Yellow Fly walked another straight line along the outside edge of my finger and continued along my hand. So small was he, that I was unable to feel his movement. Not so much as a slight tickle, yet I did not need to feel him to confirm his existence. I could see him clearly enough.

As if bored with his new adventure, he once again made the impromptu decision to release his grip on my skin and let go, this time using his skills to fly back to the window pane. There he walked up, up up again.

What did I learn from the yellow fly? I learned that nothing matters.

There you have it. I wrote all that as soon as I sat down at the café while it was still fresh in my mind, while I still felt at one with the experience, while it still felt like a thought I might want to share some day. I have written it here exactly as I wrote it at the table that day, with my pot of Jasmine tea for liquid refreshment. If I had made any amendments to it, I may have been inclined to include the fun words Hymenoptera and Lepidoptera, when denying all knowledge of small winged creature classifications. It is amazing what you can learn from a quality sit-com. They are just a couple of additions to my vocabulary gleaned from an episode of the wonderful American comedy, 'Frasier'. Never mind I did not think of them at the time so I have taken the opportunity to squeeze them in here, just for the fun of it.

I see my willingness to scrutinise the behaviour of a fly as a demonstration of maintaining my focus in the moment. It shows one of the ways I stay present. Keeping my attention in the present moment is important to me and is a skill which I have consciously practised. It is particularly valuable for my work and I like to believe is a contributory factor in the enjoyment of my reiki and massage treatments. Okay it seems like I have drifted away from buses already but then again it is all relevant. There is some indication that one of the reasons for my many encounters is my ability to be present with people.

*

One afternoon I sat upstairs on a busy number 57 moving slowly along Wimbledon Broadway. As ever I was in no particular hurry but the poor lady who sat beside me by the window, seemed quite unable to sit comfortably still, in her ever increasing state of agitation. Looking over the heads of people in an effort to assess our progress, she sighed and sighed. I looked at her and smiled. She was in no state of mind to smile back but I did not mind at all. It was then that she chose to voice her concerns. She was bothered, really bothered about how long the journey was taking and wondered what the delay could be. I had no response available other than to suggest that we were in fact moving and would "get there eventually".

This was probably not overly helpful and probably not what she wanted to hear but it was what I was thinking and worked for me, so I stayed with it. This lovely anxious lady did not want to let it go. She bounced around in her seat and strangely enough her angst did not make the bus move any quicker. I may have gently pointed this out and she told me that she just could not help it. I was comfortable and relaxed, so there on the crowded bus I said, in a not too quiet voice,

"Am I going to have to teach to you meditate to calm you down?" Well I could have had no idea how that was going to be taken but thankfully it did the trick. She stopped fidgeting and fussing immediately and even apologised for her behaviour. She then treated me to snippets of information about her little ones. Her haste was owing to her desire to return to her eighteen month old twins who were being cared for (no doubt admirably) by grandma but as time was ticking by, my seat companion was concerned that her little cherubs were possibly beginning to misbehave.

It seemed fair for me to suggest that her mother was more than likely enjoying the experience and indeed the babies might be having fun too, besides there was frankly little she could do about it from the top deck of our bus. She was a lovely lady and thanked me for my perspective and happily showed me a photograph of her offspring. Ah bless.

My work was done. It was quite easy really and all was well.

*

It was a Saturday afternoon and I was on my way home from my treatment room, sitting on a number 493 minding my own business, looking around enjoying the beauty of my surroundings and finding things to appreciate, when I heard a clicking sound. Click, click, pause, click, pause, click, click, click, pause. I ignored it at first but it continued and I only decided to pay attention to it, when I realised that the intermittent clicking was accompanied by bodily movements of the lady sitting beside me. Click, click, click, pause, click, pause ... I looked across to find her playing anatomical havoc with her phalangeal joints. Ouch! While I appreciated that they were her fingers and she had the freedom to do with them whatsoever she chose, my reverie was interrupted by her not so private activity.

I wondered, perhaps I should learn to focus better. I wondered, perhaps I should mind my own business. I wondered, perhaps she was unaware of what she was doing. I decided to believe the latter. Just for the record, I understand that there are different schools of thought concerning the effect of finger joint clicking. My medical background has always led me to conclude that it contributes to earlier onset of arthritis and common sense leads me to accept this as a viable reality. I have heard an alternative view that it somehow (I hasten to add this was unsubstantiated) that it somehow strengthens the joints. Oh really! Until I believe otherwise I shall stay with what feels right, the clicking did not feel right. She was clicking and I was distracted, my instinct was to act.

Carole Chandler

I turned towards her and without saying a word, I put my hand on her two hands, encircled my fingers around hers and gently squeezed. Well, it is one thing to speak to a stranger uninvited but it is quite another to touch a stranger uninvited. What happened next? With my hand on hers I looked at her, she stopped moving, she looked at me, I smiled, she smiled back and apologised. She said that she had not realised she was doing it and thanked me for stopping her. She had no reason to tell me but she said that the finger clicking is a habit which she is trying to break and she was actually grateful to me for bringing her attention to it.

My work was done. It was quite easy really and all was well.

*

I was on a bus from Battersea to Tooting minding my own business as we stopped at Clapham Junction and about twenty five people boarded. It is only a little single decker and it was filling up pretty nicely as we bounced along down the streets and around the commons of Clapham and Wandsworth. It was busy with many people sitting and standing, so as ever there was a certain level of, let me call it, bodily contact. I sat beside the window and the lady sitting next me was not small, so she leaned against me, particularly when other passengers passed down the gangway to get on and off. Some way into the journey, when there were less people about, I became vaguely aware of her leaning against me, perhaps a teeny weeny bit more than one might expect, even under the circumstances. I was not unduly bothered and more out of curiosity than anything else, I half-heartedly glanced in her direction. Her head was hanging down and bobbing in that easily recognisable someone-is-falling-asleep kind of way.

Ordinarily the soporific effect of the bus motion, encourages a tired person to nod off but the head bobbing generally bounces the person back to consciousness, when they sometimes look around hoping they were not noticed until the tiredness takes over again and the whole scenario is repeated. This lady was beyond this stage. Her head fell forward, her head bobbed, her arm fell on my thigh, her shoulder pressed mine on its way across my upper body. She was on her way down, so I decided that action needed to be taken, before she found herself face down in my lap.

Placing my hand on her arm, I eased her back into an upright position and asked her if she was alright. She slowly turned her face towards me and she slowly, slowly opened her eyes. The eyes that met mine were red, very red, more red than I have seen for a long time and it would have been perfectly acceptable to have felt a degree of concern for a lady with such red eyes. The uber red eyes looked in my general vicinity but I was convinced that they were not focused on me, they did not seem to focus on anything, it was simply a glazed gaze and that is all. She responded to my enquiry,

"Oh, er, yes, I'm okay, I'm just tired that's all". Her declaration of her tiredness made sense. I had witnessed her extreme tiredness, her overwhelming tiredness, her inability to stay awake and her inevitable falling-asleep-on-the-bus-overcome-by-fatigue kind of tiredness. I believed her and feeling concern for her level of consciousness and welfare, I said that I thought it might be a good idea for her to go straight home and straight to bed. Ever a Monopoly fan I resisted the temptation to say 'do not pass go and do not collect two hundred pounds'. Well, you could have knocked me down with the proverbial feather when she said that she could not go to bed because she was not going home but going to ... wait for it ... her second job! What? She had to be kidding me.

"Yes, I've been working all day, now I'm going to my other job, that's why I'm so tired and falling asleep on the bus, it's not my fault, I can't help it."

How could anyone in that condition even consider going to a second job? What on earth was she trying to do to herself? What use is the money if she has no health to enjoy it? Sleep is necessary. Sleep is restorative. Sleep deprivation is not conducive to well-being. I expressed one or two concerns to her.

"You'll make yourself unwell then you won't be able to do any of your jobs."

"I know, I know."

"Look at you, you're so tired you nearly ended up collapsing on a stranger on a bus."

"I know, I know."

"When you're this tired you get headaches, sore neck, sore back, upset stomach and you struggle to sleep properly when you do finally put your head down." While I said all this she nodded and nodded and nodded. I had said enough, I left her alone.

Several minutes later she turned to me and asked me a question. She asked me where I was from and I instinctively wanted to say that angels sent me to tell her to get some rest but I restrained myself, perhaps next time. She wanted to talk and went on to tell me that she had worked all morning in the furthest corner of north London and was travelling to the south. Her additional place of employ was to keep her busy until well into the night, when she intended to make the return journey home back to north London, to a place so far north that I had not even heard of it. She told me that it is the other side of some well-known landmark. She thanked me for my attention, she thanked me for waking her and she thanked me for my concern. I had already said one or two things about the unsustainability of sleep deprivation, resulting in the physical body complaining and ailments kicking in. She told me that she had headaches that would not go away, her sore shoulders were getting worse and her back ache did not seem to be improving either. I listened. She was already aware of the solution. I was merely reminding her of what she already knew.

Of course she had the freedom to choose to do as many jobs as she liked. She did not ask for my opinion, she did not need my opinion. I could have ignored her and kept my thoughts to myself. However, I felt guided to offer her an alternative perspective so that was what I did.

"Be careful, it is when people are this tired that they make mistakes."

"You're right, you're right, I know you're right." She told me about her children and that she planned to rest the following day which was thankfully her day off. As it was the summer holidays, I had a sneaking suspicion that her day of rest may be low on her children's list of priorities but never mind, she promised to take care of herself and that was enough for me.

We arrived at her stop, she stood up to leave, she looked at me, it was a sad look, a woeful look, I smiled, I asked for her hand, she offered it, I held her hand in both of mine, looked her in the eyes and said quietly,

"Have a peaceful shift." It may have been my imagination but she seemed to be on the verge of crying as she said,

"Thank you, thank you." Outside the bus she walked to the back, stood beside my window and waved as we drove away.

My work was done, it was easy really, all was well.

*

Yet another sleepy-on-the-bus episode presented itself, offering an opportunity for dialogue. I was on my wonderful local single decker bus and sat towards the back. First of all I call it my wonderful local bus because it provides a fabulous service which stops in the heart of my luxury new development. I am eternally grateful that I can take advantage of this service, particularly when returning late or when loaded with food supplies. Of course I could manage if I had to walk several minutes from the main road, where other routes run more frequently but I am just appreciative that I have the choice. Besides, the drivers are wonderful, friendly and helpful and I have more, much more to share about them later.

So there I was at the back of my bus one Monday around 11.30 in the morning when, for some reason, I really have no idea why but I decided to turn around and found myself staring at the woman directly behind me. She did not mind. She did not mind because she did not notice. She did not notice because she did not see me. She did not see me because her eyes were closed. Her eyes were closed because she was asleep. I was amused to see her head doing the characteristic bobbing thing. I expected her to jolt herself back to consciousness but she just bobbed and with her eyes closed, she somehow managed to remain vertical. Quite a skill I think. A skill I have never been inclined to perfect as I simply never find myself on public transport in such extreme stages of tiredness. I glanced at the man sitting opposite her, who had seen her too and we both shrugged our shoulders. I faced forward again and found things to appreciate out of the window for a while. For some reason a few minutes later I turned around again. I do not know why, I rarely do this unless I am eavesdropping on a conversation and feel the desire to join in. In this case there was silence behind me and there I was turning around again.

I turned and saw the female head bobber just beginning to stir, her eyes slowly opened, she looked at me with a glazed expression, I smiled and said,

"So you're waking up then." She grunted and looked around.

"Where am I?" Oh dear, that was not good. I gave her a location check and she looked like she was going to return to her forty winks. I was feeling playful and said,

"Would you like me to wake you up anywhere in particular?"

"No thanks, I'll be alright," and we both laughed.

A couple of minutes later her mobile phone rang and I heard,

"Yes, I know it's you, I'm sorry, I fell asleep on the bus again." Hearing her say that I turned back and winked at her and we both laughed again. A few stops later she stood up to leave. Even I was surprised when she put her hand on my shoulder and squeezed. I looked up and she smiled saying thank you. How sweet is that?

*

Moving away from sleepy heads, I feel like sharing an interesting event where a stranger spoke to me. Another time I was on a G1 travelling through Tooting on my way to Streatham for the one reason, the only reason I ever go to Streatham and that is to go to my favourite café. This glorious eating establishment not only feeds my body with divinely delicious food but also feeds my soul with its ambience. The first time I went there was with a friend and we talked and giggled for several hours. My second visit was an emotional moment for me when I tasted the soup, which I could only describe as 'love in a bowl'. My whole body tingled with each spoonful and I followed the urge to leave a note of gratitude and appreciation for the chef. I love the place so much that I have been inspired to visit regularly ever since. I focus my mind on my way there and I focus my mind on my way back. I block everything out and sometimes hardly even remember the journey. If it were not for this venue then Streatham would simply not exist.

It was on one of these bus rides when I sat at the back of the single decker bus. There were five people dotted about in front of me and seated at the front of the vehicle immediately behind the driver was a young girl, who as most people do while travelling, sat playing with some manner of hand held electronic device. I was minding my own business, idly gazing out of the window admiring the abundance of trees and the beauty of the flowers, when the young girl stood up, walked past everyone else on the bus and sat beside me. Interesting. It appeared that I had been selected for something, I had been singled out and I had no idea why until she said,

"Hallo, I'm sorry but can I borrow your phone?"

Well this was an interesting situation on a couple of levels. Firstly, this young lady had bypassed everyone else on the bus to ask me if she could use my phone, when she could just have easily asked someone closer. Secondly, I do not carry a mobile phone. I own one which I use occasionally for its calculator and alarm functions but I made the executive decision some time ago to release myself from the burden of being shackled to this form of communication. Conversations by text do not sit well with me. The common seemingly accepted practice of ignoring text messages does not sit well with me. The pattern of 'oh I'll answer it later' that I am told is the modern way, does not sit well with me. I find it singularly unsatisfactory, so dispensing with it as an option has proven to be an excellent personal decision. As for the 'convenience' of being available at any moment day and night, anywhere, at home, at work and socialising, well it is a complete nonsense. Unless one is waiting for a fresh organ for transplantation, I wonder if anyone actually needs to be eternally contactable by phone. A little time for self brings its own rewards. Paying attention to life in the moment has benefits. My choice affords me the additional advantage of being physically and emotionally present when I am in the company of another. When I am with someone I am not distracted by incoming messages, answering the phone, sending replies and interacting with someone who is not even there. When I am with someone, that person has my attention. That is what I expect from them and that is what they get from me. This all makes more sense to me and until I change my mind I shall continue to be present. An influential spiritual teacher, Theo, says *"when we are present with another they feel loved"*. The significant impact of this is that when we feel loved we feel better, when we feel better, life is easier. All is well.

Anyway, I seem to have been carried away with my little or not so little rampage about mobile phones. I have no idea what came over me and can only assume that it had to be said. Perhaps it will strike a chord with someone out there. Perhaps it may mean something to the lady I met in a shop, who one moment was peacefully browsing the selection of essential oils and enjoying the aromas when her phone rang and in an instant she cursed, shouted and lost her cool. I said,

"Oh dear, is someone trying to track you down?" She had ended her call abruptly but still retained her annoyance, she treated me to a tirade of complaints about how her family members call her for the slightest little thing, never seem to even try to manage without her, never leaving her alone for a moment, expecting her to be at their beck and call. I listened as much as she wanted, she certainly gave the impression that she needed someone to listen. When she ended with,

"I really really hate being so available all of the time." My simple suggestion that she turn her phone off, set her off again. This time she complained about how her previous attempts to do this very thing had been met with a serious lack of understanding from those trying to contact her.

Anyway, enough about her, I have said my bit and the rampage is over. It might be worth looking within and asking why I went off on one though, so note to self, do some work to make peace with mobile phones.

So back to the girl on the bus, I looked at her beautiful face, which was still beautiful even considering the streaks of mascara and eyeliner as dark tears ran down her cheeks. Yes she was crying so clearly something was amiss. She had asked me a question and I knew that what I was about to say might sound evasive. I have been told many a time by my nearest and dearest that people would not believe me if I told them that I do not carry a mobile phone. However, it was the truth, so there was not much I could do about it.

I said, "I don't carry a mobile phone so I can't let you borrow one."

"I really need to call my friend, it's urgent and I need to call her right now." I was happy to offer a suggestion. As we were driving through the grounds of a general hospital at the time, I said,

"You can get off the bus and go into the hospital, there will be phones in there."

"I don't want to get off. I just want to go straight home."

"Call your friend when you get home then."

"I need to call her now."

"Then get off the bus."

"I want to go straight home, if I get off now, I don't know how long it will be before the next bus comes."

We seemed to have reached an impasse. This poor young lady was around my own daughter's age and there is every possibility that from her perspective she was in the middle of a real, genuine, actual emergency but while I had no desire to hear any details, I put on my motherly face, I took a chance and asked,

"Is it really as serious as all that?" She sighed and slumped in the seat. The tears had stopped, she seemed a little less anxious. "It can wait can't it? Whatever it is you will be okay, everything will be okay it always is." With a much calmer physical expression about her, she seemed to understand on some level and said,

"I hope so. thank you, thank you, sorry, so sorry to disturb you."

She returned to her seat at the front of the bus and resumed her erstwhile button pressing activity on her aforementioned hand sized electronic device. She was still there when I left several stops later and with a smile and happier non mascara streaked face without tears and with no appearance of her earlier concerns, she reached out her had in my direction as I passed and thanked me again. What a sweet young lady and what an interesting sequence of events.

Something which was odd about this event was how I even came to be on that particular bus in the first place. When I left home, instead of walking to my nearest bus stop I felt the sensation to go to the previous stop, which is further away and in the wrong direction. On my way, a bus passed me. I laughed to myself realising that I would have easily caught it if I had gone to the other stop, the closer one, the more usual one for me. I laughed because I remembered that it is not possible to 'miss' a bus for if I am not on it then it is not mine. Also I wondered what might happen as a result of me not being on that one, therefore arriving somewhere at another time. Then the young girl on the bus did what she did and I wondered again about the interesting sequence of circumstances which transpired.

*

I have enjoyed seeing people sharing random acts of kindness on the bus on several occasions. A few times I remember seeing someone running, hobbling, walking quickly rushing in one way or another to catch a bus and then saw another person step into the doorway to prevent the doors from closing so that the driver cannot take off. It was only when the puffing panting person arrived that we all find out that they did not even know each other. How kind is that? I love it.

I have witnessed people going out of their way to make space for buggies and it is always amusing to see people practically tripping over each other to make a seat available for a passenger of advancing years. Talking of which, there is a sweet little lady who I have seen a few times who teaches me and perhaps one or two others a gentle lesson in humility when she boards. I have said it before and I shall say it again, that I am really not in the habit of guessing ages for obvious reasons. However this little darling has been taking part in her life experience for a good number of years and she could doubtless tell tales of historical events going back easily eight or nine decades. I have the pleasure of seeing this little sweetheart at the eastbound side of Garratt Lane at the Wimbledon road bus stop, which is invariably busy and when I have seen her it has been no exception.

When the bus arrives she hovers and someone always stands aside to allow her on before them. This in itself is not unexpected, my experience is that generally people are charming, polite and well-meaning. What always makes me smile is that she responds as if genuinely surprised. I have no idea how that is possible but surprised she is, surprised to be given the opportunity to jump the queue. Well when I say queue, I use the term loosely, this is London after all, so it tends to be more of a fragmented mass, a dispersed huddle so to speak. Anyway, more about bus queues later.

So my little sweetie boards the bus, bleeps her Freedom Pass then, wait for it … she stands by the stairs. I cannot believe that she stands as if content, as if intending to stand for the journey. Why do I find that so hilarious. I have no idea, I just do. She stands but never for long, someone often two or three people stand up and shuffle around to offer her a seat. As with the boarding scenario she responds as if genuinely surprised to be offered a seat. There is unlikely to be anyone older than her on the bus, probably for quite a distance, the fact that she travels at all, never mind by bus, might surprise some people.

I have witnessed this series of events a few times and each time I am reminded of the benefits of remembering who we are. I have no idea what she is thinking, I do not need to know, I do know that I have frequently seen people in younger physical bodies demanding and insisting and complaining about manners and seniority and respect when they tell other passengers about their displeasure of not being offered the seat, which they seem to think is rightfully theirs. Again, I can only go by the words and actions which are offered and whether I agree or not is of no consequence, the entertainment I receive from my observations is always a by-product.

So I feel the urge to return to a queuing event which led to some unexpected dialogue. I had been to one of my art shops to treat myself to a few supplies, to keep me busy with my meditation inspired artistic creations. This beautiful clean shop is in Tooting and I cannot help thinking that it feels out of place. This gorgeous haven of creativity is so unlike other shops in the vicinity. I am very glad that it is there though and the staff are quite lovely. So the bus stop just a few metres away is a convenient place to catch the bus home, or into central London depending on my plans.

So I was there one afternoon at this Bickley Road bus stop on Mitcham Road when a lady arrived and waited. I know the area well and while there is no judgement intended, I idly observed that she did not look like a local. Also, at the stop were a couple of ladies fully robed, speaking in unfamiliar words at volume to each other and to their several children and talked on mobile phones all skilfully at the same time. I know the area well and while there is no judgement intended, I idly observed that they did look like locals. They were clearly distracted both with less than happy faces, one shouting and screaming on the phone, the other continually telling her to keep her voice down.

The stop serves several routes, double deckers and single deckers, to a selection of destinations arriving often three or four at a time on a busy road in this lively part of town. People waiting need to keep their wits about them.

No one can have any idea which bus other people are waiting for, unless they ask of course but more about that later. It is really a case of each man for himself so to speak.

A bus pulled up and stopped. The two phone talking, children pushing ladies shuffled forward. The doors opened. Another bus arrived, the same ladies walked forwards and boarded the second bus. My single decker bus was close behind, so slowly I took up my position to flag it down if the two double deckers were still in situ. At the same time the doors of the first bus closed and it drove away. This was when I heard the lady behind me let out an almighty shout which surprised me. She looked really genteel so I was startled by her squeal of,

"Hey, that's my bus, he didn't wait, where is he going?" I turned to see this poor woman looking more than a little miffed to say the least. She waved her arms in dismay and looked at me in disbelief. I had seen the driver stop, I had seen the doors open, I had seen no one board, I had seen the doors close, I had seen him drive off. Where was the problem?

"Oh you poor thing, he did stop, you need to be sharper than that I'm afraid."

"I was waiting for the other two ladies to get on, I didn't want to jump the queue, they were before me and I didn't want to push in front." Oh dear, she had made a rookie mistake. Never mind, I think we all make that error at least once, I know I did and like me she will probably learn not to let it happen again.

"It's not queue jumping, this is London, particularly as you have no idea which bus they were waiting for. Anyway there'll be another bus soon." She was not ready to be consoled just yet, so she continued,

"Thank you but I'm really angry now." To be fair she had a point but I knew that her being angry was an option that would be unlikely to get her very far in that moment.

"Don't be angry, it's a lesson I learned the hard way too. Besides, there is probably a very good reason why you were not supposed to be on that bus." I decided to leave her with that thought and not involve myself any further. With all of this going on I had to be savvy and make sure that I did not 'miss' my own bus. It came, I was on it, we left, all was well.

This meeting was not unlike an experience that I had when I waited for a number 9 outside Charing Cross station. At the bus stop there was the familiar crowd of people waiting for any of the many buses which pick up there. As before, no one knew which bus anyone else was waiting for. Unlike before the bus was unlikely to fly past because of the amount of traffic and there is always someone getting off.

What happened on this particular day was that a bus stopped and people moved from several directions across the pavement to board. A couple of ladies openly expressed indignation at what they considered to be queue jumping, and how people have more manners from their home town 'in the North'. Oh dear, Londoners were getting a raw deal again, I thought of defending us locals and decided against it because in those circumstances, what would have been the point?

*

For some reason, I am also reminded of a lady I had a chat with at the Wimbledon theatre bus stop on Wimbledon Broadway. I was pretty happy as I had just bought tickets to see Starlight Express which is just the best musical ever, so in my excitement I waited for a bus back to our shop and treatment rooms.

I had not been there long when a woman arrived. She told me she was breathless from walking quickly all the way from South Wimbledon which is about fifteen minutes away. I had not asked her but she volunteered that she had chosen to walk because there was an accident around the corner, buses were not getting through, ambulances and police cars were present and crowds were getting in the way.

I was not unduly concerned so I told her that I saw no reason to leave. Interestingly, this lady chose to stay and talk to me when I said that I was happy to wait. She was terribly well spoken and complained a bit about her plans being interfered with and shared her thoughts about the unreliability of buses and wondered if she should have taken another route. I simply smiled and calmly said,

"You think you're having a bad day, what about the person that the ambulance was for?" To be honest that is not the kind of thing I would say often but it felt right at the time. She seemed to lighten up in response and said,

Carole Chandler

"Oh yes, if you put it like that I can see that I really have nothing to worry about."

"Just offering another perspective," I added.

"Thank you very much for helping me to see things differently." That was sweet of her to say so but she really had no need to thank me. As it happened a bus came within a couple of minutes so we were soon on our way.

*

Talking of perspectives I found myself at a bus stop on the Blackshaw Road beside St George's Hospital in Tooting. I say found myself because I had no good reason to be there. Travelling from Wimbledon, I had followed the irresistible urge to get off the 219 early at the Longley Road stop and then walked out of my way, around a corner and down the road to be at a bus stop, which seemed to offer me no real advantage. What was I doing there? I could have just as easily stayed on my earlier bus and got off at the Broadway and walked. Alternatively I could have stayed on and walked along Burntwood Lane, the picturesque scenic route beside the golf course, if I felt so inclined or I could have crossed over at the Broadway and caught a bus straight home. These options made more sense. I could have made one of these seemingly wiser choices but I did not, I simply felt guided to be somewhere that was inconvenient and made no sense. Anyway, I have learned not to question my instincts, all I have to do is follow them, I know they serve me well and it can be fun seeing how circumstances turn out.

I had stopped wondering why I was there and after several minutes of watching the world go by, an elderly gentleman walked purposefully to the bus shelter and immediately asked me if I had been waiting long. Ooh, now there is a meaty question. I could have had so much fun considering the notion of time and the illusion that is time and the idea of comparing the longness or shortness of something which is as real as we make it. Talk about perspective, wow. A long time for one may be a short time for another, so how can a person walk up to an absolute stranger and ask if they had been waiting for a long time? What can that question ever mean?

Perspective is a wonderful thing and an example which springs to mind is when I sat upstairs on a number 38 leaving Piccadilly, passing Regents Park on our way to Victoria. I had a clear view out of the front window and enjoyed my journey as we travelled smoothly on a gorgeous day with a normal flow of other road users. As far as I could see all was well. I was surprised to hear a couple behind me complaining to each other about how annoyingly long the journey was and how they hated London traffic and how they wished they had taken another route and how they wished there were less cars and how the delay was upsetting them and other insignificant irritations. I found it hard to believe that we were on the same vehicle. There was no traffic from my perspective, no delays, we were flowing nicely. As if to prove me wrong, a lady in front of them then had a conversation on her phone complaining about the slow bus, delays, traffic and more. Perhaps I was never going to understand. My journey was fine, theirs was not and that was all there was to it. I have a sneaking suspicion that this may not be the last time that I say that 'it is all about perspectives'.

A chap I had known for a considerable number of years asked me a question a while ago. It was a simple question really, after we had a minor disagreement on some national economic issue, he asked,

"Do you live in an alternative universe?" The conversations I overheard on the number 38 reminded me that the answer is obviously, yes.

So back to the Blackshaw Road bus stop and the question which required a response. I was feeling playful and probably would have enjoyed the entertainment of a lively debate about the illusion of time but the furrowed brow of the gentleman before me, led me to suspect that it might be prudent to just temporarily buy into the concept of human dictated chronological measurements. I surmised that by saying, "no, not long", that he could assume it to mean whatever he wished. I did not mind either way.

He inspected the timetable, he inspected his watch, he looked at each again, then tutted and muttered. Oh dear, he was not a happy bunny. I gave up with timetables a long time ago, after all this is London. Generally buses are fairly frequent but it would not be reasonable to expect them to arrive as a timetable dictates. Apparently, others think differently and that is fine too. He said,

"The 493 is due in a minute." I could have left him with the thought which seemed to give him comfort. For some reason I said,

"I have just seen a 493." Well, according to his calculations that should not have happened and he said,

"Did you miss it?" I have already said my bit about the prospect of how we may 'miss' a bus so I shall let it go. When I said no he asked,

"Aren't you waiting for a bus then?" What a question. Why would I be sitting at a bus stop but not be waiting for a bus? Clearly I had much to learn. When I told him yes he sounded confused when he said, "you said you saw one."

"I did." I paused and his look of increasing confusion led me to continue, "I'm not waiting for that one." Suddenly he remembered that the stop serves another route and laughed saying that he had forgotten because he was concentrating on his own. What a sweetie.

He asked if I worked at the hospital and I said no but I strongly suspect that he would have continued to say what he continued to say regardless of whether I worked there or not. He wanted me to know that it is not just a good hospital but an excellent one, somewhere at the top of the list for care in the country. Not only that, he wanted me to know that it is the best in Europe for heart conditions, to use his words 'it is the best heart hospital'. He seemed happy to talk and without any enquiry from me, he told me that he had a cardiac incident three years ago and they looked after him and he is grateful to them for being alive today and without them he would not be at the bus stop with me. He seemed happy enough chatting away partly to himself, telling me how highly he thought of our local general hospital and I felt content enough to hear it. I was not bothered by his declarations and had no intention of disagreeing with him and equally felt no inclination to agree either.

This sweet gentleman had a fair amount to say, then made me laugh hysterically when he asked me one of the funniest questions I have ever been asked. I have no idea why I found it quite so amusing, I just did. I laughed so loudly that people across the road looked in our direction to see what the noise was about. I fear I was far from ladylike but he caught me totally by surprise when he asked,

"Have you heard of Margaret Thatcher?" Oh dear, it is making me laugh again just thinking about it. When I finished rolling around the bus shelter in hysterics I desperately wanted to know what on earth he was thinking, that led him to ask such a question. I asked him a couple of times but sadly we will never know because unlike me at that moment, he maintained his focus and proceeded to give me a detailed account of his views of our former prime minister. If I was not already aware, he was making it his job to educate me about political affiliations, historical proposals, hospital closures and his involvement in prevention campaigns and blah, blah, blah.

This gentleman was quite passionate and I am convinced that any contribution from me would have simply fuelled his already blazing flames. Anyway, I did not care enough to join his single person debate. I have spent a considerable portion of this lifetime devoted to the enjoyment and endurance of employment in the NHS and I have heard every angle of every discussion and frankly I am glad to have no part of it now. He told me what he thought, I did not really listen and I am not sure that he actually cared.

When my bus stop companion transferred his attention from general NHS specifics to his personal specifics he said that he was told that his chances of survival were fifty fifty. Well I was still feeling playful, so I said that this is the same for everyone. He stopped talking, looked at me, thought about it and said that apparently I had made a good point.

Suddenly and it felt really sudden at the time he said,

"I want to go to Sri Lanka but I can't." It was so sudden that I briefly wondered if someone else had joined our conversation. Okay, I thought to myself, I can go along with his train of thought and see where it leads. To me, the uninitiated, it seemed that he had changed the subject, however it turned out that he wanted to go on holiday and he had been warned against it for reasons to do with air travel, temperature and his health. He really wanted to go, he was used to going every year and he was missing it. His wife had gone without him for the past three years and he was feeling left out. He talked about accommodation, flights, expense, food, heat, humidity and rain. He worked himself into a bit of a paddy as he talked himself into it, then it seemed to talk himself out of the whole idea of going at all.

I looked at him, I smiled, I said, "You worry a lot don't you?"

"Oh why do you say that? Is it my face, is it the way my face looks that makes you say that?"

"It's what you're saying, I'm listening to you and so much of what you say is worrying about something or another."

"Well, I'm a pensioner that is what we do, we worry about things."

"You say that you want to go to Sri Lanka, then you listed lots of reasons why you won't go which are nothing to do with someone else telling you not to go."

"I was just thinking about things."

"What do you want to do, would you like to go or not?"

"Yes, I really want to go."

"So go then."

He wanted to go, he really wanted to go and he knew it would make him happy to enjoy a holiday in his favourite part of the world. He remembered returning from previous visits when friends and family told him he looked younger. He remembered feeling rejuvenated by the air, the sea, the trees, the flowers, the people and the food. It was a joy for me to hear him talking positively about the reasons for going, his little face had lit up and he seemed excited.

"So what is stopping you then? Worry is the only thing preventing you from doing something that you know you will enjoy." He seemed hell bent on looking for excuses and returned to the subject of finances. He could not say that he did not have the money, he could not say that he did then he talked about financial commitments. What was he doing to himself, worry, worry, worry, why, why, why? As for the money, it would be no use to him if he had another heart attack and was no longer around to spend it, regardless of whether he took his vacation or not. I gently pointed out that his worrying may well put him back in hospital. I offered an opinion and said that it made no difference whether he went or not but to make up his mind one way or the other, be happy with the decision and stop worrying about it.

"I've decided I'm going. I'm going to go before Christmas, the weather will be right then." His expression softened, his eyes looked brighter, he made his decision, his bus came and he surprised me by saying,

"Thank you, thank you for letting me talk to you," then he disappeared off into the sunset. Seconds later my bus came as if it had been waiting for the correct moment. Why had I made the detour to put me in that place at that time? I wondered no longer. For people who believe in coincidence, I shall leave them to think that our meeting was simply a matter of chance. My knowledge has taught me that there is no such thing as coincidence, so I continue to be amused by every interaction.

*

Another interaction with an elderly member of our population began at the bus stop outside TKMaxx at Clapham Junction. There were several people waiting as usual scattered around in the shelter, behind, in front and beside the stop where half a dozen routes stop on their way to a variety of destinations. When my bus arrived, a dear sweet old lady moved forward and asked me if it was my bus, before I began to move. I guessed she just wanted to talk to me. The door opened and she insisted I board before her, which was interesting because our older travellers tend to enjoy being acknowledged the grace of seniority, allowing them to take their place before others, as a matter of simple courtesy. Anyway, she insisted and I was not about to argue with her so I stepped up, bleeped my card, greeted the driver and walked to the very back seat to sit by the window. Well, blow me if this sweet little dear didn't make the trek to the back of the vehicle, hobbling with her stick to sit right beside me. Once again, I was amused by the proceedings because there were other seats available and yet she joined me and right beside me. Interesting.

She smiled sweetly and asked me where I was going, telling me that she liked that particular bus route because it took her directly to the hospital which meant she did not have to walk. I was pleased for her and would have been quite content to end our interaction right there. My new companion had other ideas, she wanted to talk about the shortness of her life, her advancing years, her approaching demise and particularly about how when she goes she cannot take anything with her. I suppose these thoughts were heavy on her mind because I requested none of it and yet she seemed to blurt out her thoughts quite easily.

I said something about leaving things behind for other people to enjoy and she mentioned a television programme about people who apparently had no family members, no heirs, no one to inherit their fortunes. I could hear that talking about it was not bringing her joy, so I asked her how she feels when she watches that morning programme.

"I don't like it, I don't like it at all, it really upsets me." I softly suggested that she watch something else that feels better. I do not know what she thought because she said nothing. Perhaps she was thinking. Not for long though because she distracted herself with complaints about people, television, crime, good people and bad people. I felt no desire to question her views on any of these because she had her opinions and they were all fine. However, she wanted to talk and she wanted to include me, I could not join her because I do not share her perspective. I have trained myself to pay attention only to things which please me. I have learned from wise teachers that *we get the essence of what we think about, whether wanted or unwanted*. When she asked me what I thought, I said what I believe, that everyone has the right to choose.

My companion was not impressed, that was okay with me. I understand that some people think this way and most do not. She quoted something from her religious book, said a few things about bad people and where they are going, then pointedly ignored me for the remainder of the journey.

This was an interesting interaction initiated and concluded by this dear sweet little old lady.

*

Sometimes people really like to talk on buses, often they include me and I am grateful for the occasions when they do not. One Sunday morning on a 295 in Clapham Junction, me and the other passengers found ourselves enjoying or enduring (purely depending on your perspective) a full blown preaching session. Our impromptu speaker was a lady wearing a brightly coloured voluminous blouse and skirt. After her loud singing, she quoted religious passages directing her attention for that moment at teenagers and her opinion of sexual behaviour among the unmarried. She had a lot to say and our bus was her pulpit.

I was new to the area and vaguely wondered if I was to expect this as a regular Sunday morning transportation entertainment treat. Anyway, luckily she seemed content to speak and sing without directly involving individuals.

*

That event was in contrast to another journey where I travelled from Highgate to Kings Cross. The bus was full and a lady at the back seemed to be talking to friends sitting with her when I boarded. I sat a couple of seats in front of this rather vocal lady, minding my own business. Well I tried to mind my own business but she was hard to ignore. I learned during our journey that she did not know these people but she had latched onto them because she was sharing her joy of Independence Day for her country. She appeared to target her attention at passengers of colour, assuming interest based on presumed nationality. She invited them to join her celebrations somewhere south of the river.

I tried not to laugh when she issued her invitations because she admitted that she did not know where she was going, had no address, nor start and finish times for the festivities. I understand that the timing was less relevant as often these unofficial affairs tend to be somewhat fluid in their organisation but I guessed that at the very least a location would be required.

This lady's vocal chords received little rest as she educated us all on some aspects of her country's history, their oppression under the rule of a European power and how independence has improved the nation, except for the fact that her people have insufficient food or money.

She did practically all of the talking. She singled out a few people and asked them what they thought. One or two responded, she seemed happy to talk. I was content to not be included. The route terminated at Kings

Carole Chandler

Cross, everyone got off and she stood up wishing each person a happy Independence Day as they walked past. Interestingly, when I walked past her I smiled and she simply said,

"Thank you sister."

*

I remember a time when I was particularly singled out for conversation. On a beautiful sunny day leaving Clapham Junction heading towards Clapham South, I sat to the rear of the bus beside the window, minding my own business, looking out admiring the beauty of anything that I saw.

A small boy in grey t-shirt and shorts with delightfully unruly blond curly hair skipped towards the back of our single decker bus and ignoring other available seats, he sat beside me. I did not notice who he was with but with surprising confidence he sat sideways next to me with one leg on the seat, his knee facing me and a foot tucked under his other leg dangling below. He was perhaps three years old and looked like a wise man in miniature. I looked at him and smiled. He looked at me and with hardly any expression he said,

"I like to sit by the window." He continued to look at me as if awaiting a response. To say I was fascinated by him would be an understatement, however in the moment I decided to just say,

"Do you?"

He maintained his fixed stare and added, "Yes, I like to sit there." This little man sounded quite determined and the last thing I wanted was for a situation to erupt. I quickly considered my options and taking a chance, I went with,

"Oh well, never mind, perhaps next time." Luckily for me he instantly responded with,

"Okay", adjusted his position to sit with both legs and his body facing forward and his feet off the seat. Well this little boy seemed very sure of himself indeed. I glanced around again to see who he might be with but no adult seemed to be looking for him nor was he looking for anyone else. For someone so young he was not only happy to continue sitting beside a stranger but he was happy to continue talking.

"Are you going home?" he asked. I told him I was.

"Where have you been?" he asked. Well I am used to strangers striking up a conversation with me but this was a teeny weeny bit out of the ordinary even for me. I answered him somewhat amused by his maturity. Then blow me if he did not start talking about the traffic. Seriously, was he for real?

"I thought there would be more traffic here today. They were digging the road up yesterday and it was really bad, lots of cars waiting. Today it's much better. I thought the road diggers would be here, I like diggers, I like watching them. I've got diggers at home. I like to play with them. Do you like diggers?" I could hardly believe what I was hearing. He barely paused for breath and was absolutely adorable. He happily chatted away until we turned a corner, when he jumped onto his seat to see better out of the window and shouted,

"Oh here they are, the diggers are here and there's Roly!" In his excitement he had suddenly lost me for a moment so I enquired,

"Roly?"

"Roly is the steam roller, he's Bob the Builder's friend, he helps Bob the Builder." Ah, then I understood and I loved how he had hurtled himself into a subject more age appropriate.

Before I had the chance to respond, not that I needed to as he was happy enough expressing his own thoughts with minimal interaction, he turned his attention to the front of the bus and announced,

"This is me," climbed down from his seat and walked to the door. Yes he actually said, 'this is me', not 'this is my stop' or 'I get off here' or 'time for me to go', he actually said, 'this is me'. I was intrigued by his manner, his behaviour, his confidence and still wondered who was in charge of him, though he appeared to be more than capable of taking care of himself. The mystery was solved when I saw him jump off the bus closely followed by a lady pushing a buggy with a smaller equally blond and fabulously curly haired male child. My earlier companion skipped along the pavement beside them and I was delighted to see that he was still chattering. How wonderful.

Who knows, perhaps one day his younger sibling may delight a lady on a bus with his powers of observation and communication, I expect so.

*

Children on buses are great fun. I remember sitting upstairs on a number 38 leaving Victoria on our way to Piccadilly and a woman sat at the front with her little girl. She enjoyed the journey and described her view out of the window with such enthusiasm and infectious laughter that it reminded me about the benefits of viewing the world through the eyes of a child. In the words of the wonderful George Benson *"let the children's laughter remind us how we used to be."*

She did not care how many buses she saw, or trees, or bicycles or lorries or doors or flowers or shops or men or hats or dogs or pigeons or anything it seemed. This adorable little girl excitedly mentioned them all, like she was seeing each one for the first time. I loved it. I loved hearing her joy. It is probably fair to say that her mother's enthusiasm waned considerably during the journey but never mind we all had fun in our own way. Listening to this sweet little darling was fun for me and it made my day.

*

This reminds me of another day when I had the honour of witnessing the power of a small person on a bus crowded with adults. I was on a single decker towards the back and in the middle by the window stood a little girl probably about two years old perhaps less, certainly young enough to be still happy with life and not care what other people thought about her. She bounced around on the lap of her accompanying adult and spent the entire journey waving at each and every person on the bus. Some people noticed her, some did not. Some people waved back, some did not. Her enthusiasm did not seem to diminish either way, she waved with or without a response. As for her smile, well it lit up her pretty, cute, little face. She smiled and waved and appeared to be having endless fun.

This little girl's persistence in spreading love and joy paid off. Her accompanying adult took no part in the smiling and waving activity by the way and this was fine too. The little cherub was freely allowed to interact with us without interruption. By the time they got off, several people were waving back merrily to the cutest girl in the world. She waved her way from the vehicle and along the pavement as she maintained her attention on us.

Make no mistake about it, she may have been small, she may have been young but this little lady had the power to promote a fun atmosphere in the bus which persisted after her departure, as people talked about her glee and joie de vivre.

*

The pleasure of this little girl was a direct contrast to another small person who struggled to make himself understood by his adult. As far as I could see he was not totally content with the instruction to sit in his buggy, he expressed a clear desire to sit on the lap of the lady with him but this was repeatedly denied. Of course no one can be certain of her reason except that she was attempting a conversation with someone on a mobile phone and the boy's requests for attention seemed to cause something akin to minor irritation.

There ensued an ever increasing contest and if I were a gambling person, my wager would have been with the boy. He continued to refuse to be seated where he did not want to be. The mother's instructions consisted of 'sit there', 'sit down', 'don't do that', 'do this', which needless to say were all ineffective, then I was amused when she raised her game to 'I'm warning you', 'do I look like I'm joking', 'I'm not messing about', 'I mean it', 'I really mean it'. Still with neither of them satisfied, she continued to bark at him and he continued to express his preference for her lap over the buggy seat, even when she announced that when they arrived home, he would be 'going on the naughty step'. He made a fuss, she made a fuss, they were both persistent in their fuss making. A couple of people made it their business to tut their disapproval, I sat directly behind them and had a clear view of the journey's goings on.

When at last she picked him up and at last put him on her lap, he was already complaining and crying so loudly that it seemed he was too far gone to be consoled. Who knows? All I know is that he wriggled and squirmed on her legs, perched on his knees, looked over her shoulder, looked at me, stopped crying, stopped fidgeting and responded to my smile with a big grin. He put his head on her shoulder and closed his eyes. It was lovely to see him finally find an emotionally peaceful place. Whether it was necessary or not for the whole commotion to have taken place, is not for me to decide, I guess that ultimately all was well.

That contrasts nicely with a lovely journey I remember when two little girls boarded excitedly with their mother after what they told me was a 'brilliant' day at school. The confident talkative ladies aged five and seven, as they joyfully told me, were really happy to talk to me. Their mother was quite delightful and said that her daughters love school and are great company for each other playing nicely together at home. I was pleased to hear it and it was a joy to meet them. Interestingly, the mother spoke kindly to them and they spoke kindly to each other.

*

There have been times when I have witnessed behaviour on buses which have made quite an impact on me. Perhaps I have not spoken to the people involved and they have not spoken to me but I have learned something about communication.

A major learning experience for me a few years ago was when I saw a woman on a bus with a beautiful black glossy coated Labrador. The lady sat on the seat in front of the exit door and her dog sat beside her on the floor. I observed her taking care of him, moving him out of the way as passengers passed, particularly ensuring that his tail was safe. Of course that is the very least an owner would do I suppose, anywhere with pedestrian traffic, however for me it was the way the dog responded to her movements, her attention, the way he looked in her eyes, the way she looked at him, the gentle way she handled him and repositioned him. I remember being fascinated by watching the two of them together.

I clearly remember making a powerful discovery, it was as if witnessing tenderness between two individuals for the first time. I said to myself, "Ah, so that must be what love is." Perhaps I was witnessing tenderness between two loving energies for the first time. The point is that I had probably seen it before but not realised what it was. My recent personal development work had brought me to a new and improved emotional place, where I could actually recognise love, affection, grace and many more wonderful aspects of human interaction. If I had seen people displaying affection in the past, my default setting was to want to stick my fingers down my throat. Those days are long behind me, however it has taken some relearning. Bearing in mind that the lady with the dog on the bus experience was only about five years ago, that gives you some idea how far I have come, not to mention the significant work which has been done.

*

Another profound learning experience was when I sat in the rear of a busy double decker somewhere along Regents Street in London. Several people were standing and they gave the appearance of being a group of individuals just standing and waiting. The double seat in front of me became available and a young well-dressed gentleman quickly moved to take the position by the window. Almost at the same time a young lady sat beside him. It occurred to me that it seemed odd for her to move that quickly, until I realised that she was not just sitting next to him but also looking at him. She looked at him but he did not look at her. He stared forward. I did not want to but I felt uncomfortable.

It looked odd because they did not appear to be together, yet she continued to look at his face and he continued to studiously avoid looking at her. What was that all about? She put her head on his shoulder and he turned his head away to look out of the window. Perhaps he was a graduate from the 'treat 'em mean, keep 'em keen' school of romance. Perhaps she was looking for something which did not exist. She nuzzled or at least tried to, by which point I chose to assume that they knew each other. Presuming that they were on some level acquainted, it was a strained relationship that I was witnessing. Cold shoulders and nuzzling do not go together. I should know, I have tried, I have been there. Feelings were welling up within me as I observed them. I was reminded of too many similar circumstances where I have attempted to find comfort from a place where attention and affection were not available to me.

I started to feel sorry for her, then to take myself away from thoughts of my unhappy past, I reminded myself that she is fine, he is fine, they are together learning and teaching whatever is appropriate at the time. If they are right for each other, then they will work it out. If they are not right for each other, then they will work it out. Either way their experiences are helping them to determine what is right for them and as long as they follow their own inner guidance, then all is well.

I have regained my self-empowerment and enjoy the personal freedom which comes from understanding that I do not need to worry about anything which appears to be an injustice. Now I am open and available to seeing beauty and positivity in all things.

*

I saw a lovely couple travelling closer to home on my local single decker bus. They were quite unlike my previous couple of urban young professionals who were fashionably well-dressed with a corporate look about them, not stiff black suits, just business like. Anyway, unlike them these two were of advancing years, well into retirement and paid a considerable amount of attention to each other with a vast amount of affection being openly displayed. He kissed her, they said a few words, she kissed him, they said a few words, they kissed each other, they said a few words, they kissed on the lips, on the cheeks, on the hands and this was how they carried on pretty much throughout the journey. Now I realise that this gives the impression that I stared beady eyed at them throughout the trip. Well, I do not think I was glued to them but they were in front of me and it was kind of sweet and they did not seem to care and I do like to see people in love and I do like to see people at least being nice to each other and … well … it was lovely. Perhaps another day another time another place I might not have even noticed them, who is to know? In fact who cares? It was lovely and I learned a lot once again. It would be easy to assume that their open displays of affection were an indication of a new and budding romantic association, perhaps it was, I like to think it was. As it happens, I can choose to believe whatever I like, so I choose to believe that they adored each other whether they have known each other for five months or fifty years.

*

It is nice to know that relationships can be loving even after the first throws of youth and when the wheels of lust have stopped turning. I was in the changing rooms of the Rohan store in Covent Garden last week, trying on some necessary performance clothing to comfortably protect me and nurture me through the fast approaching winter months after our glorious summer weather.

I overheard a conversation between the lady in the cubicle opposite and the gentleman sitting on a comfy seat outside. They too were well into retirement and during my wanders back and forth, I had already smiled at the chap and received a lovely smile in return. I had also made a comment to the lady and she agreed that the trying on and shopping for clothes is sometimes not so easy.

From inside my cubicle with its rustic wooden barn door, I heard them interacting with such caring, loving, sweetness that I stopped feeling sorry for him for shopping with her at all in the first place. Come on let's face it, there are few chaps of the boy meets girl persuasion who are actually keen on shopping for women's clothing. The whole process of trying on this and that, asking for opinions, compliments, honesty, guidance and whatever, can be understandably quite tiresome. Most guys in those circumstances are on a hiding to nothing, often whatever he says leads to some manner of misunderstanding. This does not apply to the man I overhead in the Hobbs clothes store in Chelsea's Kings Road. He had no such problem and disagreed with all of his girlfriend's decisions and choices. Openly ignoring her preferences he actually said to a member of staff,

"She thinks she wants the red one but I know she will look terrible in it, so get her this in black." If that is caring, then I do not care for it. Suffice to say, I did not stay long. My focus abilities were being seriously hampered by hearing him.

So back to the Rohan barn cupboard, the lady showed the gent and he sweetly talked her through options, asked her what her preferences were, he sounded like he actually cared, he listened to her. It is a long time since I have heard such patience in a clothes shop and if the wonderful comedian Jason Manford is anything to go by, I am not alone. I could not help myself. I had to say something. I joined them and smiled, the lady spoke first,

"Oh I hope we weren't being too noisy."

"No not at all, I was just enjoying listening to your conversation"

"Oh really!"

"Yes, it is so nice to hear how lovely you are with each other."

The chap laughed and said, "What, you mean arguing all of the time?"

"That's not what I heard, no arguing, you are really nice together." They looked at me a little bemused. I thought that maybe they had recently met, perhaps they were the result of some budding romance or a new dating encounter and were planning a romantic trip to a lakes and mountains location.

I asked, "Have you known each other long?" There was a short pause before the lady said,

"We met when I was 15 years old and that was 53 years ago, we were childhood sweethearts." I was genuinely surprised. There was no way I would have guessed that and I was delighted for them. I am quite aware that there must be couples who have been together for a long time and still behave lovingly towards each other. I walked along the seafront in Devon's pretty area of Torquay on a cold wintery morning and saw an abundance of elderly couples walking hand in hand. It would be nice to think that at least some of them still like each other. However I am also quite aware that many people go their whole lives without finding a partnership like the fitting room couple, not for even a short time. Is it too late for me to dream of having an experience like that? The dream continues. Dreaming has value.

When I had picked my jaw up from the floor I said, "Oh bless you both, that's wonderful. How amazing that you've known each other for that long and still speak so lovingly towards each other."

He said, "Oh I don't know about that, we have our moments, it can be a bit up and down."

"Of course," I replied, "that makes sense but going by what I overheard, yours is a loving caring relationship." They both looked surprised but found the space to say thank you. I did not want to interrupt their shopping spree any longer so I said,

"It has been an honour to meet you."

As I walked way the chap said, "It was nice to meet you too."

This sweet couple has probably forgotten all about it but our encounter has made quite an impression on me and has helped me to imagine more wonderful relationships coming my way.

I meant what I said, meeting this lovely couple felt like a privilege. They reminded me of a beautiful lady who works in a lovely café which I like to visit. I loved hearing about how she and her husband have been together since their teenage years and how they continue to adore their time together, after four children and nearly thirty years of marriage. It was wonderful to hear about his attention and affection for her recent birthday celebrations and all went a long way towards making me assume that she is possibly married to one of the most thoughtful men ever. The only reason I found out any of this was because one Monday lunchtime, I walked into the café and she looked not just beautiful but radiant, she glowed so brightly that I felt the impulse to tell her so. That was when I had the pleasure of hearing some of her weekend activities and joyous they were too. I thought of her when I met the changing room couple and vaguely imagined her and her husband being like them in years to come. When I was next in the café I told her about them and she amazed me with even more sharing of love and romance.

Her parents have been married for forty eight years and the previous weekend her father danced her mother, his wife of all those years, he dance her around the room early in the morning singing to her. Yes, he was serenading her to celebrate their anniversary. Oh my goodness, I was so touched, I thought, I really thought I was going to cry. I felt the lacrimal glands beginning to overwork in response to my emotions and it was all I could do to stop myself from blubbing right there at the table. I managed to contain myself only to discover that the dawn dancing and serenading were not the end of it. There was more. Every year he writes on the back of her card, I love you. That is lovely is it not? Wait for it … he writes those three words in kisses. Oh there I was again, practically being tipped over the emotional edge. The tears were on their way again. I mean really, he writes I love you in kisses on the back of her card every year. I felt so happy for them both, not only that, I felt happy for the lady who was telling me this lovely sweet account of attention and affection. So after all these years, I am finally beginning to understand what Joan Armatrading was singing about. Her beautiful song 'Love and Affection' used to be just words, now it has meaning.

I thanked the café lass for telling me about her parents and their loving expressions towards each other. I felt honoured to hear it. I also told her that her relationship with her own husband made more sense to me, after hearing that she and her siblings had grown up in a loving caring family where expressions of affection were openly displayed. As I told her I have only recently discovered that this emotion even exists. Of course I have seen the movies and I thought that some of the scenes I saw were just that, only things which happened in movies.

That is quite enough about that, time to move on.

*

Make no mistake, I have had more than my fair share of people saying wonderful things to me in a variety of places including on buses, at bus stops and generally around events involving bus travel.

Standing at the Wimbledon Road bus stop on Garratt Lane in Wandsworth I was minding my own business looking around for things to admire when a man appeared from my left and instead of walking past, he stopped in front of me. Well, that is not a first but it is a source of wonder to me every time it happens. As he was right in front of me, I could not have avoided him even if I had wanted to, so I looked at him and smiled. What I did not expect him to do was to just stand there. Also what I did not expect was for him to say,

"Wow, you are so beautiful." Ooh what a lovely thing for him to think, let alone voice out loud, not just to anyone but to me, to my face, how lovely. I thanked him. He continued to stand right there in front of me, he continued to stare, he said,

"I swear to God, you really are." Well, I vaguely thought to myself that as declarations go he sounded pretty sincere, or at least I liked to think so. I was happy to receive his compliments and his gaze of wonder was initially received with gratitude but he seemed to think nothing of remaining rooted to the spot on the pavement with his fixed stare on his object of attention, which at that precise moment appeared to be moi.

It seemed only fair to both of us for me to break his trance and after a few words of appreciation from me in honour of his welcome praise of me, I gave him permission to be on his way and enjoy the rest of his day. Who am I kidding? Perhaps I could have stayed there all day being told how beautiful he thought I was. Perhaps I was too hasty in dismissing him. Oh well, perhaps next time. Just for the record I have learned so much and come such a long way that I have discovered that there is always a next time.

I passed the Fairlight Road bus stop off Garratt Lane in Tooting and a guy stepped out from the bus shelter to stand in front of me and tell me he thought I was beautiful. How sweet.

Then there was the guy at the bus stop in Wandsworth who followed the impulse to do the same thing. Then there was the guy in the supermarket ... then there was the waiter in the restaurant ... then there was the lady on the pavement ... then there was the woman on the bus ... then there was the cashier in the supermarket ... there have been a few, well there have been several. Well alright, here have been lots. It has laughingly become commonplace. I say laughingly not because I find it comical, I do not think that at all, I love it, who wouldn't? It is laughable that I am the same person who until about three years ago would have struggled to remember a single occasion where anyone called me beautiful. Well that was then and this is now and I am enjoying it. Make no mistake I am no Naomi Campbell, I am just me but the change has come about following my conscious decision to change the way I view myself and the way I speak about myself. As if by magic people seemed to have changed the way they view me and speak about me too. It seems like magic indeed.

These new experiences are all a far cry from the time I stood under the bus shelter on Park Lane beside our beautiful Hyde Park, when a chap approached me and ...

Stop Carole stop, what are you doing? You know better than to tell that story. Yes it may prove to be shocking and yes everyone is likely to agree with you that the events which transpired were indeed unpleasant and there is no doubt that the random act of unkindness was unprovoked and so on and so forth but you know that you will do yourself no favours by sharing it here and now. Perhaps it is possible for you to tell it and stay in a good feeling emotional place but is it worth the risk? You know better than that, you know much better than that. For now congratulate yourself for stopping in time and grabbing yourself back from the brink of a negative place for the sake of storytelling. Note to self, remember to share good feeling thoughts, remember to pay no attention to thoughts which do not please me, remember that they do not serve me or whoever I am talking to and at this moment that means you.

I nearly went there but that was then and this is now. My experiences are utterly transformed. How is it possible that random strangers now think nothing of complimenting me and being so lovely and kind to me? Whatever the reason, I know that it feels good.

*

Another time another place, it was a Friday lunch time when I found myself approaching the turnstile to avail myself of the facilities at Victoria coach station, when a chap in uniform approached me and said,

"Hallo, I suppose you were wondering why I was staring at you." Oh bless him, I had no wish to hurt his feelings but I had not noticed him looking at me at all. The poor man may have been watching me but if I had seen him on some level, then I had not felt anything unusual in his presence. I am so accustomed to people looking at me that it now bothers me not one bit. It used to bother me. It used to be a huge problem for me. When people stared at me before, I assumed there was something wrong with me. I assumed it was for a negative reason. Thank goodness that changed. Believe me those limiting beliefs are simply not conducive to well-being. That was before I allowed myself to be me. That was back when I did not understand myself. That was back when I did not understand how the world works.

So the unformed chap wanted to talk to me and I did not have the heart to tell him I had not noticed his attention so I just smiled. He continued,

"I sat behind you on the number 44 bus on my way to work this morning."

"Oh really, you remembered me?"

"Yes, I remember your hair, I was admiring it on the bus and I am glad to see you again to tell you how lovely it looks." Well that was a surprise. I mean really, I was on that bus several hours before then on my way to my regular Friday morning meditation meeting in Covent Garden. Considering where he worked, he must have seen hundreds of people pass by, yet he remembered little me. Also, he would have been on that bus around half past six in the morning, at a time so early that it is safe to assume that most passengers notice very little. I have travelled often at that time and there is always a snooze like feel about the place. I usually feel like I am the only person awake and alert. Anyway, it appears that this sweet man was awake and alert and found both the time and the inclination to enjoy my hair. I thanked him for noticing, I thanked him for remembering and I thanked him for taking the trouble to mention it. I felt blessed.

*

Perhaps it is something about the place because I enjoyed another interaction with another member of staff in the same place. I travel a lot by coach, I like it and in the last couple of years I have been to several places around the country departing from Victoria coach station. The services are surprisingly efficient. They always leave on time and often arrive early. I sit in peace and comfort and the on board facilities surprise me by turning out to be better than I expected.

I could not help noticing a handsome, jovial young man who works in the station and always enjoyed his pleasant manner, cheerful nature and helpful attitude. I have seen him assist with luggage, offer change for the machine and generally help to make life a little easier for travellers passing through. Prior to my departure for a couple of days on the south coast I saw him again and decided to make the interaction more than the usual pleasantries.

"Hallo there, I've seen you here many times. Do you never have a day off?" He laughed a sweet laugh and seemed happy to tell me his work schedule. I told the female colleague standing beside him that I had seen this chap before and always enjoyed his smiling face and happy nature. She said he is always like that, which I readily believe. They asked if work was my reason for travelling through so often and I gave them some of the reasons for my frequent visits here and there. I shared with them that on that day, I was off to Bournemouth for some winter walks along the beach. The lady told me it was too cold and I assured her that I had plenty of warm clothes with me.

79

Carole Chandler

On my way back out again the lady was busy elsewhere, the young man seemed about to say goodbye but instead asked if I had read something in a newspaper. Well as I stopped reading newspapers a few years ago, my answer was easy. He picked up a tabloid from the desk in their office to show me the front page and I stopped him before he could go any further.

"No, I have not seen it because I don't read newspapers."

"Shall I tell you about it?"

"Well is it a happy story, will it make me feel good?"

"Er, I suppose not but it …"

"I don't want to hear it."

"Everyone is talking about it. You won't be able to avoid this one."

"Yes I will." He thought about it and put the paper down again. I continued, "I thought so, I guess if it is on the front page of that paper it is likely to be something unpleasant. That is how they sell papers and that is how they draw people in. I choose not to read about things like that. I choose what I read, I choose the music I listen to, I choose who I speak to and I choose where I spend my time."

He said, "Wow, I wish I could be like that."

"Well, I think you are already like that on some level."

"I mean be able to avoid that kind of stuff."

"I get the impression that you are doing it some of the time. I have seen you here many times and your happy disposition shows that you must already be like that on some level, which is one of the reasons you stay so cheerful." I mean it, when I say that he is one of the happiest people who I have met and whether he is aware of it or not, it takes some kind of focus for him to be like that.

*

I met another chap who gave the impression of being happy in his work. I was out on one of my evening strolls on my way to one of the local parks when I saw a London Transport van parked beside a bus stop. On the pavement was a man wearing a high visibility jacket and he smiled and greeted me as I walked past. I wondered if he was changing a poster but saw that he was cleaning the bus shelter. I just assumed that he was on a mission to make some unwelcome graffiti disappear. I returned his hallo and walked on.

On my way home a little while later, I was surprised to see him again on the opposite pavement as I walked back down the same road. When I asked him if he was sent to magically remove something unwanted from the walls, he told me that he regularly cleans the bus shelters. That is his job. I was surprised because I have never seen anyone cleaning them before and had no idea that it was a regular activity. He was friendly and seemed happy and we talked about his work. I thanked him for doing a fabulous job and left him smiling and cleaning. He was a lovely man and I was happy to meet him.

About a year later I was on another one of my evening strolls and I idly wondered to myself that I had not seen the bus shelter cleaner since that meeting. I wander the local streets often and it seemed odd that our paths had not crossed again. Just for fun I felt in the mood to take a new route. Then, lo and behold as if by magic, there was a London transport van parked beside a man cleaning the bus shelter. Not sure that he was the same guy, I asked him if he remembered our chat the previous year and bless him for recalling our meeting.

We had a longer conversation, I enjoyed listening to him tell me how often he works his route and the area of roads that he is responsible for. He was a man happy in his work and it was a joy to be in his company. I thanked him again for keeping our bus shelters in good condition and walked on. Bless him, I have spoken to people in professional careers who did not sound nearly so content.

*

Moving on to a different subject, another time another place, I found myself one weekday afternoon standing opposite St Leonard's church in Streatham waiting for my bus home. I probably do not want to get too carried away talking about this particular bus stop because if I lose focus I am likely to not feel so good. Suffice to say that this location is a particular challenge and I have since discovered that the next stop on the route is like being in another town, perhaps even another country and it suits me better to wait there instead.

Anyway, there I was, as ever it was busy. It is always busy. It is quite common to see thirty people waiting in a variety of collections of singles, couples and groups scattered around the pavement and this day was no exception. I chose to take up my position against the railings on the wall where several other people waited. There were spaces along the same wall, so imagine my amusement when a chap walked from the shelter directly towards me. He put his bags on the floor by my feet, stood sideways beside the railings and faced me.

I know that on such a wide pavement, with such a long wall and so many places where he could have chosen to park himself, that there must have been a reason why he had decided to stand next to me. I turned to look at him and was further amused by his cheeky grin. His opening line was,

"Do you mind if I stand next to you?" I had no problem with it so he continued,

"My bus is coming in six minutes so I have six minutes to behave myself." That was an intriguing way to open dialogue and it begged the question,

"Is that a long time for you then?" He made me laugh when he said,

"Well that depends, I'll do my best." I could have asked what it depended upon but I did not feel in the mood for one of those goading cat and mouse kind of conversations. I used to get involved in them but I do not enjoy that kind of interaction any more. To be honest I did not really enjoy them then but took part in the spirit of endeavouring to enjoy the company in which I found myself at the time. They rarely end well so now I leave them for others. Besides, I had a sneaking suspicion that his cheeky, playful grin had given him away already and perhaps he might not last that long at all.

My new wall companion sported a scarlet face, an unkempt appearance, scent of tobacco and the aroma of stale alcohol. He retrieved a can of lager from his bag, telling me that he had purchased a six pack for his evening meal. Then he interrupted himself by saying,

"You are very beautiful." Okay, that was nice of him I thought to myself.

"I hope you don't mind me saying that." I wondered why he thought I might object.

"Some women don't like strangers talking to them." I said something about people responding differently depending on their experiences.

"You don't mind me talking to you then?" I said that if I minded I would tell him, so until then he was probably okay.

"I'm an alcoholic." I told him I was aware of that.

"Sometimes people don't like it but you are still letting me talk to you?" I told him it was no problem for me.

 84

"I'm not drunk right now, honest I'm not drunk now." I told him that it made no difference to me whether he was or not and that I thought he had the freedom to choose. He paused and seemed to be thinking about something. He asked me where I had been and where I was going, I followed my guidance to respond with non-specifics. His swift jump from the general to his direct enquiry about my marital status caught me a by surprise. As I was not entirely sure where he was going with his line of questioning, I responded vaguely. He looked at my left hand and due to the absence of finger decoration, he decided I was single, which I thought was amusing. It was funny to me because back in the days when I wore an engagement, wedding and eternity ring, people did not believe I was married then either. How hilarious is that?

He said, "You're married to yourself aren't you?" which I thought was an interesting thing to say and it sounded about right so I felt happy to agree with him. He took time out to rummage in a few pockets and said,

"I'll tell you what, if I give you my card you will have my number so perhaps you could give me a call." I already knew that on many levels this was not going to happen. Perhaps he did too because without pausing he said,

"You could give me your card and then I'll have your number and perhaps I'll call you or perhaps I won't." I have had some funny conversations and this one was turning into a very comical one indeed, so of course I burst out laughing. What was he saying such an odd thing for? Well I soon found out why,

"Come on don't laugh, I'm trying really hard here, I'm not very good at this, I'm trying to ask you out on a date and you're so beautiful you must be asked out all the time." I stopped laughing and waited. He continued, "Look at me I'm an alcoholic and I'm thinking that I don't have a chance with someone as beautiful as you." Well, they were his words not mine, how was I supposed to respond to that? I simply smiled. He was clearly not disheartened much because he asked, "So do I have a chance then?"

Oh dear, I did not want to hurt his feelings but it was time to bring this conversation to a conclusion. I thought about it and said,

"You're not in my vortex." That was me being truthful to myself. I saw no benefit in focusing on the aspects of him which made any invitation impossible to accept. I chose an explanation that made sense to me. What I did not expect was for him to take a step backwards, throw his arms up in the air and shout,

"Oh blast, every time!" What did he mean by "every time"? Had that been said to him many times before?

I do not believe that he understood what I said and I would be very surprised if he understood what I said the way I meant it, perhaps he did not need to. His own understanding was sufficient. My daughter laughed when I told her about this interaction,

"Oh mother, did you actually say those words to a total stranger?" She knows that this expression 'in my vortex' is used often in my spiritual journey and means the place of faith where all of my perfect people, places and experiences are to be enjoyed. As I told her, they were the only words that truly reflected my feeling at the time. To have made up some other excuse would have been insincere and not fair to the cheeky grin guy. My bus arrival was timely, that is it came immediately so we parted company and all was well.

*

The stop where that all happened is not a place where I choose to wait any more. It is far too frantic for my liking. It serves several routes and I have grown less inclined to find enjoyment from being an active member of this apparent battle ground in the necessary mobilisation, which takes place every ninety seconds. I seldom find it fun to be part of the assembled masses endeavouring to make themselves visible to the driver of their approaching machine. This is interesting enough if just one bus appears, so imagine the commotion when three or four buses rock up simultaneously. I know that I love London and I know that I love buses but that particularly place and its prospects are not my idea of fun. I shall leave it to people who especially enjoy it or more to the point, do not know any better.

My solution is to walk just a few minutes to the next stop where I have the pleasure of a usually empty seat, perhaps one or two people may join me, I have grass behind me, the beauty of Tooting Common in front of me. There may be a queue of cars on their approach to the lights but the whole experience is much calmer and exceedingly more preferable to the hectic melée at the aforementioned location.

So at my new relatively tranquil spot, I was joined by a chap who smiled at me and said hello as soon as he arrived. I thought that was nice of him. He opened the dialogue with an observation about the recent change in our London weather. He was right, it was cold. He was right, it had suddenly changed. He was right, we had enjoyed some lovely hot sunny days. As it was September I sincerely hoped that he was not right when he said,

"We'll be singing Jingle Bells soon." I laughed and expressed the hope that we might have a few weeks before the persistent background carol singing was upon us. I love the festive music but the thought of it beginning this early, might test even my conscious approach to put a positive spin on things.

He sat with me and mentioned the cold again, not complaining just observing I think and making pleasant though unnecessary conversation. He said,

"I have lived in this country for a long time, so I'm used to it. I've been here more than fifty years." I guess that might be long enough to become acclimatised to the weather of any part of the world. He said that when he first arrived from his hot country, the cold winters here were a shock to his system. I was happy to listen to him. He went on to tell me that he worked in banking in London for over twenty years. I have no idea why he felt the impulse to tell me all this but I was still happy to listen. His bus arrived before mine and he left with a cheery smile and,

"It was nice of you to talk to me, thank you." Interesting.

Our conversation reminded me of a couple I met recently in a shop in Covent Garden when we found ourselves chatting about the expectation of winter. The girl reminisced about her familiarity with minus thirty degree snowy months in her home country of Lithuania and the guy made us both laugh when he confessed that he has lived in London for three years and his first two winters were such a shock that he thought his "ears were going to freeze and fall off." Poor love. Anyway, back to the bus stop.

Meeting the banking carol singer reminded me of a gentleman around the same age who joined me at the Fairlight road bus stop opposite the tyre fitters on Garratt Lane in Tooting. It was early on a Wednesday and I was on my way to my therapy rooms in Wimbledon. He walked purposefully in my direction, stood beside me, smiled and began speaking immediately. I mean, how cool is that? What a compliment it is when people who do not know me, strangers in our busy multicultural capital city, are happy to start conversations with me so openly and so readily. Come on, we all know what it is like, when we see others we scan, we assume, we judge, we decide. When I made significant changes to my life, I received the welcome bonus of people noticing me and I understand the huge compliment that it is when people talk to me. I am blessed.

This sweet old man told me that he had just been swimming and was feeling good. He went on to tell me that he swims every weekday morning and this has been his routine since retiring five years ago. Oh bless him, he sounded pretty pleased with himself and rightly so. I suspect he enjoyed the feedback and attention he was receiving from me because during the few minutes we spent together, he told me that he does all of the cooking at home, that his wife has not had to do any throughout their marriage, that he is devoted to his wife, that she is very beautiful and he tells her so every day, that in their advancing years together she becomes more beautiful, that she is the best mother, that he is proud of his children, proud of the lives they are leading, that they have great careers, that they live in large houses, that he adores his grandchildren, that he came to this country with little money, that he had no skills, that he hardly spoke English, that he managed to change all that and improve his life and that he was keen to maintain his fitness to enjoy the rest of his life.

This lovely man spoke quickly and excitedly, hardly pausing for breath. I could try but it would be difficult for me to adequately convey the joy and enthusiasm with which he told me all of this. He was clearly a man who was happy with his lot. I was happy to hear it, all of it, I was delighted for him and

Carole Chandler

his wife and his family. It was great to hear him express his contentment, well done him and his love for his nearest and dearest. Oh my goodness, how long were we at the bus stop? It was not long at all, it was just that he used the time well.

*

There was another occasion when I was treated to another information filled conversation with a stranger at a bus stop. An unusually well-dressed trim lady walked towards me with hair tied back neatly, wearing quilted jacket, tailored trousers, neck scarf, modest make up and noticeably elegant hands. After a shared smile and hallo she told me that she was on her way home following a routine eye appointment. She used to make the trek to North London's famous Moorfields but now is happy to be seen by an equally proficient ophthalmic team in Tooting.

Before I go on, I feel the temptation to attempt some clarification. In case I have not made it obvious, I would just like to mention that when I meet this variety of people I do not ask them where they have been. I mean really, why would I? They are strangers, we do not know each other. Consistent with the definition of a stranger, we have never met before and may never meet again. I do not ask them for details of their journeys, their lives or activities, they just seem to want to tell me.

So this time was no different and my new bus stop companion was keen to chat. As ever I was happy to listen. Little did I know that I was in for a special treat. I really sat up and paid attention when she told me that she used to live off Leicester Square in a fifth floor apartment facing China Town, where she enjoyed the Chinese New Year celebrations from the comfort of her home. How great is that? She actually lived there and I thought it must have been fantastic fun. She confirmed that it was fun and proceeded to share more stories about how Cambridge Circus used to be a roundabout and there was a driving school nearby, which she went to when she decided to learn to drive. She admitted that she enjoyed living in such a central location with fantastic public transport right there on her doorstep but she decided to learn to drive when she became fed up with, as she put it, "being repeatedly chucked off the tube", due to the proliferation of incendiary devices dotted about the capital with alarming regularity at that time. I loved hearing about how she drove around Trafalgar Square before there were traffic lights. She had to be kidding me, that must have been a long, long, long time ago, how could she be old enough? I did not ask her but she seemed happy enough to disclose her age and I had little success in hiding my disbelief. Suffice to say she looked con-sid-er-ab-ly younger than the number she offered.

Oh bless her, she was telling me about life, which I have only had glimpses of in old movies. Her stories were wonderful and colourful. She regaled me with her memories of Covent Garden market, as it used to be, full of flowers with fruit and veg stalls where the Transport Museum is now. She told me about life in the old market before it moved to Vauxhall, like the time when a French lorry got stuck in the place where the jewellery stalls are now and how she guided the driver out because she just happened to speak French. This wonderful lady had lived in Paris when their market moved location too and she jokingly wondered about the coincidence of living in a similar apartment in two similar cities with similar markets which met similar fates. I am sure it was nothing to do with her at all. Obviously, she had many stories to tell, I was enjoying the company of a lady who had clearly lived a full life, I told her that if she wrote a book about her experiences I would love to read it.

I am not joking, I could have listened to her all day. As chance would have it we waited ages for our bus, far longer than any timetable would have the audacity to suggest for an inner city service, yet she seemed happy enough and I found no reason to complain because she was so much fun to chat with. Meeting this wonderful lady was a blessing, a blessing indeed. So enthralled was I by her anecdotes that I did not even think to ask about her noticeably elegant hands.

*

I had another interesting yet much shorter interaction with a young lady beside a Trafalgar Square bus stop. I was walking past when she stopped me and asked if I would help. I am always willing to be of assistance when the opportunity presents itself and I saw this as another occasion for me to briefly wonder why she had chosen to ask me, instead of one of the other one hundred and fifty people who passed her on that busy pavement at the same time as me. Okay, okay, okay, I admit that perhaps my estimated figure may be an exaggeration but not by much. I imagine that where we were standing, outside an embassy, across the road from Horatio's Pillar, it would not take long for a hundred and fifty people to walk past anyway.

The lady was trying to make sense of the map in the bus shelter and frankly I often find them more confusing than not. They can be particularly irritating when they claim to show stops, directions and routes but often leave us travellers none the wiser. I live in London and I find them troublesome, never mind this poor lady who had flown in from Munich. She was quite delightful with a pretty cheerful face and bright eyes and she seemed very happy to tell me that she had made the trip to London to visit a spa that she had discovered. She was planning to come over once a month to enjoy the benefits of the great feeling that the treatments and facilities gave her.

Wow, it must have been a really good spa to entice this German lady to leave her Munich home to travel to London on a regular basis to reap the benefits. We both laughed and chatted easily and agreed that it is great to find somewhere that we really like to relax and restore our batteries. It makes the journey worthwhile.

It would be safe to assume that I asked her the name of the spa, so that I could try it for myself. After all I live in London, so would not even have to factor in the cost of air fare and hotels into the equation. Yes that would be a fair assumption but no I did not ask. Why not? I have no idea, I just did not think of it at the time, so I was none the wiser after I pointed her in the right direction for her bus journey.

*

It makes sense that people will ask for help when travelling, it makes sense that they will ask someone who looks like they may know the answer. Perhaps I should not wonder why I am asked so frequently for directions, perhaps it should be obvious to me but I do still wonder and it is a continuing source of amusement to me.

Sometimes people approach me and ask and other times I see someone looking perplexed and instead of minding my own business and looking the other way, I take advantage of the opportunity to offer assistance. Either way it is all the same to me, if I can help I will, if I can't I won't and if I didn't want to I wouldn't.

So there was the time I was outside the massive Sainsbury's on Tooting Broadway, just around the corner from the tiled wall of the underground station and the statue of Edward VII and the flower stall with its gorgeous array of colours and arrangements and the beautiful Victorian green sign posts and the pretty multiple street lanterns. Just for the record, these are the aspects of the vibrant traffic light junction of Tooting Broadway which I choose to pay attention to. I make a conscious decision to look for something beautiful to admire, anything attractive to appreciate, a hint of joy to focus upon when I am passing through.

I could easily choose to observe the pedestrian activity, the doorway dwellers, the often less than inspiring human interaction but there is an associated risk of being drawn away from my good feeling emotional place. Yes, I can get back there, yes, I know what to do to get back on track, yes, I can remember to focus but why make life hard for myself? I choose what I wish to observe instead of observing that which I do not wish to see.

So the bus stop had a huge gathering of people and there was nothing unusual about that. I was sitting at one end of the red seat and there was something very unusual about that. Firstly, it is rare for me to find a space to sit there with the many people who gather there wanting to wait and rest with their bulging orange carrier bags. Secondly, if I do decide to be there, I generally prefer to find a space away from the main huddle, rather than place myself in the thick of the collection of bodies and bags. Thirdly, I rarely wait here anyway, as I made the happy discovery of catching my bus, two stops before this location, in relative bliss. In that particular area the stops are really close together so I plan accordingly. I think ahead when changing buses, if and I say if I shop in that store, I visit early, whizz round, get out quick and go home. As for the changing buses lark, I shall just explain that Tooting Broadway may be known to some and unfamiliar to others but until I moved here, I had absolutely no idea that it is such a hub for the London bus network in the south. They go to so many places, admittedly to places I have no intention of visiting but it is easy to get into the centre too. We are well catered for. Most people praise it for being on the tube line but as I have not been on an underground train since the morning of the Millennium celebrations, the subway form of transport is of little interest to me.

I realise that this is a radical life style choice for a Londoner but it is my choice and serves me well. Years ago a friend expressed, how shall I put it, er … let me just say, dissatisfaction with my desire to travel above ground. Yes, yes, yes, I know that 'it is faster by tube' but like I definitely said in my first book and like I probably said in my second, come on folks, what is this obsession with speed anyway? Besides, time is an illusion. I prefer to enjoy my journey, see where I am going and interact with the driver of my transport but more, much more about that later.

Oh yeah, back to the speed thing, I am sometimes reminded of the negative side of underground travel when I stand upstairs at a station for whatever reason, perhaps waiting for someone's arrival, topping up my travel card, passing through or just for perverse morbid curiosity. It can be a real surprise to remind myself of the vast numbers of people and the pace at which they fly through the exit. There are invariably so many people moving so fast and for what reason?

These are some of the same people who come to me as clients for emotional rest, physical recuperation and for restoration of spiritual balance. I have said my bit, give me a bus, I am happy to sit upstairs or downstairs and take my time. I had a friend who was quite dismayed when I told him I would rather travel an hour by bus than twenty minutes by tube. So what, I leave earlier and give myself more time. What is the big deal anyway?

Funnily enough I have found that because buses have to travel in 'traffic' and their timing is inevitably unpredictable, perhaps that is not quite fair, it would be more accurate to say that even with their published timetable the journey time is perhaps predictable but indeterminable, anyway for this reason I give myself plenty of time, often ridiculous amounts of extra time and I am rarely 'late' as a result.

I have witnessed humorous conversations where people endeavour to plan their underground journeys to the minute. What kind of a life is that? I shall tell you what kind of a life that is, it is a stress inducing life, that is what it is.

Phew, breathe Carole, breathe. Excuse me a moment, just hold on while I climb down from my soap box. Let me allow myself to return to the more usual calm not bothered about what other people do or how they choose to live their lives person that I prefer to be. Wow, that was quite a rant was it not? I can only assume that it needed to be said. I felt guided to go off on one, so shall trust that it was the right thing to do. If just one person makes a decision to slow down even a little as a consequence then hey, all is well.

Back to the conversation at the bus stop, a lady was giving directions to our local hospital. She told the two enquiring women which buses to get on. It was really none of my business and I have no doubt they would have been fine eventually but they were being given inconclusive information. Yes the options she gave them did go past the hospital but she omitted to tell them which number goes around the grounds to the various wings, entrances and so on. The direction giver was loud and not someone I felt inclined to openly contradict, so I left her to it.

When one of the enquirers glanced in my direction, I quietly beckoned her with a little nod and a small 'come hither' of an index finger. She came over from the other side of the bus shelter past all the people who stood between us. Even this made me laugh to myself because she could have had no idea why she had been summoned by this quiet stranger at the end of the bench, yet she came anyway. She confirmed that they did want to visit the hospital itself, so I quietly told her which bus would definitely serve their needs. I wanted the same bus so when it arrived we all boarded. I sat at the back they sat in the middle.

Now then let me just get a little something off my chest. I decided from the outset to include the locations and route numbers in my book so that anyone who does know the area might get an extra kick out of my anecdotal sharings. At the same time, I fully appreciate that if you are reading this in a North American suburb or a Devonshire village or even on an Australian beach, i.e. anywhere outside London then the specific road names and bus numbers are of little consequence. However, it is the essence of my tales which I would hope you find the space to enjoy. Just substitute my city for your city, my town for your town, my road for your road, my details for your details. I like to think that they are transferable. If not (because let's face it there is only one Covent Garden,) just enjoy the interactions wherever they may be. More to the point, if there is another Covent Garden somewhere else out there in the world then I would sincerely love to hear about it

Now in the world of our current location, the bus on this particular route has not just one but six stops related to the hospital in question, so it is quite understandable that there tends to be an element of confusion, when people are unfamiliar with their destination. I had already established the requirements of my two ladies, so from my central rear position on the bus I was able to observe them clearly. At the first opportunity they turned to look at me for clarification. I slowly shook my head and they remained seated. At the next stop they turned towards me again with an enquiring look and again I slowly shook my head, once again they remained seated. This happened once more and each time I surprised myself just a little bit more by the amount of trust they seemed to have in me. Why oh why did they put so much faith in this quiet person at the back of the bus? I was just a person who they did not know, who claimed to know what she was talking about. Interestingly, the previous direction giver was considerably louder and gave the impression of being knowledgeable, well that is if volume is any indication.

When we finally approached the correct bus stop for my ladies, the one in charge turned towards me, I smiled, I nodded, I gestured, the bus announced confirmation and they seemed to happily disembark. They walked past the nearest window to me and with bright smiling faces, they waved enthusiastically. I felt blessed. I felt blessed indeed that they trusted me so much. Of course, I know it would not have been the end of the world if they had got off two or three stops early, it really was no big deal. It was just nice to be instrumental in making their day a little easier.

*

There was a similar incident which filled me with delight when I travelled on a 493 from Wimbledon to Tooting one day after a session of treatment giving. A woman sat at the back of the bus and discussed her business so loudly, that not just me but everybody knew that she was meeting someone at Burntwood Lane in Earlsfield. It is one of my local roads so its location is no mystery to me. She was talking to a friend sitting beside her, who barely said a word, not that she really had a chance and not that she needed to. The loud one spoke enough for both of them it seemed.

There had obviously been some discussion between her and the driver before I joined the entertainment because when we approached Gap Road he called out to tell her to get off, directing her up the hill towards Southfields. She stood up and started to walk past me towards the door. Well excuse me for not minding my own business, excuse me for being nosy, excuse me for knowing the area and excuse me for wanting to help. We were far enough away from the aforementioned lane, for me to be on the verge of witnessing a gross injustice, which I could avert if I chose to involve myself. I chose to involve myself.

I put my hand on her arm as she walked past me and said quietly,

"You said you are going to Burntwood Lane, this is a long way from there, stay on the bus, I'll tell you where to get off and I'll direct you." She was really quite sweet, a sweet lady who shouted when she spoke. She made the whole bus laugh (well perhaps not the driver) when she returned to her seat and said, (loudly of course)

"My friends keep telling me to keep my voice down but sometimes it pays to have a loud voice. At least you know where I'm going." I could not help responding,

"Darling, the whole bus knows where you are going." Luckily she laughed and was not the least bit offended. Well, why would she be? I spoke affectionately with love from the heart.

Once again a total stranger trusted me. I would have quite understood if she had chosen to ignore me and followed the advice of the driver, that would have made more sense, after all he was the expert. The difference here was that I knew what I was talking about. I am loathe to say that he was wrong because however we choose to look at it, even if she had got off way too early and walked up the hill in the wrong direction, she would have stumbled across her intended road eventually, perhaps a little frazzled, perhaps a little angry, perhaps altering the entire rendezvous with her friend perhaps, perhaps, perhaps. Never mind, no one knows what the outcome might have been. All I know is that she stayed on board, left when I indicated and thanked me for the directions I gave her for the final section of her journey.

Once again I surprised myself a little more by the amount of trust she seemed to have in me. Why oh why did she put so much faith in this quiet person on the bus? This person who she did not know who claimed to know what she was talking about. On neither occasion did I offer any qualifications such as living locally, frequently travelling the route or any other reasons why they might choose to take more notice of me than the other person. I felt blessed. I felt blessed indeed that they trusted me so much.

*

Sometimes the whole direction giving thing can be unintentionally complicated. I remember walking along Plough Lane when a lady got off a bus across the road from the petrol station. She asked me how to get to Wembley Stadium. Oh my goodness, she had to be kidding me. Wembley stadium is the other side of London and given time I could probably work out some kind of vague route or at least I could get her headed in the general direction, giving her the option of asking again when she was closer. However, I was put on the spot and expressed my surprise at her attempting to bus her way to Wembley from south west London. Luckily for her my surprise triggered something in her thought process because she suddenly revised her request from Wembley Stadium to Wimbledon Stadium. Oh well, that made much more sense. She wanted the Wimbledon Stadium dog racing track and luckily for her we were right outside. Very lucky for her that I did not send her miles out of her way to her mispronounced location.

*

Another time I was given an opportunity to help I waited for a number 44 in Victoria opposite the supermarket. As usual lots of people were waiting for lots of buses to lots of destinations, when a family of two adults and two small children walked towards us. Out of all the people in the scattered huddle, the father chose to stand in front of me. I smiled. He said, "Shepherds Bush". That was all, just those two words, Shepherds Bush. They were non English speakers, so after some pointing and gesticulating he seemed to suggest that it was his family's intention to go to Shepherds Bush. Oh dear, my knowledge was not enough to help them but I knew a man who could. I left my waiting zone and led the four of them with their massive (really huge) suitcases, through the crowd, around the corner, through another crowd to the terminus information office.

All I had to do was say to the bus network uniformed chap that this family wanted to find their way to Shepherds Bush and he flipped his lid so to speak. Apparently they had already met him and he had spent ages with them, given bus numbers and directions and he was fed up with them, so he sent us all away. How interesting for me to observe his alternative approach. Luckily another member of staff was a tad more agreeable, the family went their way, I went mine, returned to my stop and my bus came immediately, so all was well. I would have struggled to stay pleasantly positive if I had seen a 44 pulling away as I returned but I would have just had to remind myself that if I am was not on it then it was not my bus. Anyway, that did not happen and the timing was perfect.

*

Then there was the time I walked out of Victoria coach station when as I left the building I walked towards the traffic lights, a boy aged about ten years old walked past several people to stand in front of me and asked if I knew the way to the passport office. Anyone who has ever visited Victoria coach station during daylight hours for travel or any other reason will know that crowds of people milling about in the doorway is a common sight.

Well I am often surprised to be so singled out and this occasion was no exception. Firstly, his age made me remember how children are so tuned into energy and follow their instincts far more readily than adults. Their understanding is more natural for them and children approach people they feel drawn towards for energetic reasons without doubting themselves or their decision. Secondly, he seemed to be on his own. Where was his accompanying adult? When I asked him, this young boy pointed towards a woman a few metres away, sitting on luggage and she did not look well, she did not look well at all. Perhaps I was too hasty, perhaps she was feeling better than she has felt for a long time. However, my initial impression of her went some way towards explaining why the boy was doing the asking.

*

Now then, teenagers are another ball game entirely. I remember saying in my previous book that they are often asking questions and receiving inadequate answers, so find themselves in the midst of strong emotions, they know they do not feel good, they are not sure why and they dig their heels in as a result.

My own dear children have been wonderful teachers for me not least during their teenage years. Seriously, ask any parent of a teenager whether life is easy with this age group. If they say yes then great, if they think not then they will have a great number of parents who agree.

Ooh ooh ooh, this feels like the perfect place to slot in a little tale about a lady I met in Richmond Park. I had never met her before and she was with a lady I had not seen since our early journey into motherhood. My acquaintance made small talk and as she had similar aged teenage children, she asked about mine. When I said that my children were great, the stranger scoffed and told me that I was lucky.

Lucky! Lucky! What did she mean lucky? This was a few years ago and I did not know then what I know now, so her remark touched a nerve. I found myself asking why parents are to blame if a teenager is challenging (for want of a better word), yet the parent is lucky when a teenager is conforming (for want of a better word). That makes no sense, it cannot be both, either we are responsible for both or we are responsible for neither, opinionated onlookers cannot have it both ways. I told her that I was not 'lucky' to have great children, that they were wonderful and it had nothing to do with luck. Perhaps they were great because there was a teeny weeny possibility that I might have, just might have done one or two things right as a parent. This was a new perspective for me anyway because I had spent the majority of my early parenting telling myself that I was rubbish at it, especially when we were struggling with behaviour patterns. Ring any bells anyone?

So here I am now with a whole new, positive, life enhancing view on the world around me. I feel blessed to have two children who know how to follow their instincts. I understand that their choices may not be choices which I would make. I understand that their choices are none of my business. I understand that it is not my job to override their inner guidance. They have no interest in following my spiritual journey, they have little patience with my desire to consciously live to the laws of the universe, yet they live them unconsciously. They are a classic example of how cosmic law works for everyone, at all times, on all subjects, without exception, whether they believe it or not, whether they understand it or not. In the process, my wonderful children have taught me without even realising it. How? Well, if I can focus myself into a place of positivity and joy when they are displaying behaviour which is less than joyous then I know I am doing well.

I am choosing not to give specifics about behaviour and attitude, we all have examples of our own, I do not think that any reader will benefit from hearing mine. Suffice to say, challenges call for greater focus, greater focus leads to feeling better, feeling better creates positive results. We teach by example. Our children learn by example. Teenagers rarely learn from our words anyway, they have an admirable skill of being able to successfully switch off when the words begin. Ask any parent, teacher or someone endeavouring to assume authority. This is one of the reasons I offer examples in my book, so many examples of my life, my changed life, my life where I am finally allowing myself to be me and let others be as they choose to be.

Enough about all that for the moment, time to move on.

*

One day I sat towards the rear of a single decker bus and at the very back tucked away in the corner sat a dark foreboding figure of a young man aged around seventeen. I would just like to point out that I do not make a hobby of guessing or estimating people's age or weight as it happens for obvious reasons. However this young man looked about my son's age so merely for the purposes of my anecdotal sharing, I am choosing to slot him in my teenagers category. If by some fluke he were to ever recognise himself among these pages and if I have estimated wrongly then I hope he will forgive my placing. He may well be a large twelve year old or a youthful looking forty year old but I doubt it. He sat wearing a peaked cap, hood up, dark clothing, sprawled on the seat not looking particularly like he was interested in engaging with anyone. Well, why would he want to? For most of the beginning of our journey he was quiet and I was pleasantly unaware of him and I imagine that he was pleasantly unaware of me too.

We were close to my destination when we stopped in traffic, for longer than usual on a triple lane one way street. I heard music playing, so glanced across, saw windows open and as we were not moving, I guessed that the music was coming from one of the cars alongside us. The music was nice, I quite liked it, so feeling playful I began to sway, nod and move my shoulders to the beat of the rhythm and blues version of a well-known song which was playing.

When the music began it would have been easy to drop into the common adult perspective of complaining about the younger generation, passing opinions on the consideration for others or even questioning the action of imposed listening. I may have been guilty of all of these responses back in the day but not now, not any more. Now I live much more in the moment and base my decisions on my current thinking instead of how I used to think or what I assume others are thinking or of what they might think of me. Another time, another place who knows what my reaction might have been. All I know is that at that time, in that place the music sounded good, I liked it, my body wanted to move to it so I moved to it. Did I give any thought to what anyone else on the bus was thinking? Not much.

A woman sat in front of me and on her lap knelt a little girl aged around five-ish who had been passing the time with me making faces, smiling, winking and hiding behind her fingers for part of our journey. When the little one saw me having a little jig along to the music she joined me dancing from her lap position. The music was good and the little girl was having fun with me, yet I think we were both a bit surprised when her mother joined in with a little bop of her own, particularly as beforehand, she had repeatedly told her daughter to sit still. So there we were, the three of us having a cheeky little shared musical moment.

The R & B number stopped and was replaced by something okay but not nearly as tuneful, so our dancing ceased. The new track was getting louder, we were still 'in traffic' so I glanced across again to see if the music was coming from the builders on a house across the road, perhaps they were making their day a little more fun with some tuneful accompaniment. Something made me look back, right back and there in the corner was the aforementioned dark, hooded, (yet now not nearly so foreboding) figure. He was sitting up pressing the screen of some manner of hand held music playing device. It certainly looked like an iPhone to me but I do not claim to be an expert. What did surprise me was that he had it pressed against the window and seemed to be operating it from that position. I have since been informed by my own resident teenager, that it is a well-known fact among the fraternity, that these machines play louder and clearer when held and operated against the pane of glass on buses. Well there you go. I had learned something new and witnessed the evidence of it.

So I had turned back, seen the music was coming not from outside but inside our vehicle, courtesy of our young man, who looked up and saw me openly observing his activity. I have no idea what he thought, I did not need to know. I have learned that it does not help to worry what others think about me, it only matters what I think about them. That is where my power is and it is not exclusive to me, this knowledge gives each of us our power back. I have also spent sufficient time with teenagers to learn the value of disregarding their visual countenance, which may give an unintentional negative impression. My work, my goal is to offer love from my heart. Now that I feel this love for myself, it is easier to offer it unconditionally to others.

I looked at him and smiled. I felt warm and happy, so smiling was easy. It was an impulse, I simply followed my inclination to smile at the busy, music playing, dark figure in the corner with no consideration for how he might respond. I did not know whether to be surprised or not when he smiled back. His whole demeanour changed, the dark figure seemed suddenly bright, the peaked cap no longer cast a shadow and his smile lit up his handsome face as he raised his head to continue looking straight at me. On reflection it was a beautiful moment.

I turned my attention away, the music continued, the lady and the little girl in front were quietly facing forward too and all was well. Finally our bus progressed through the traffic lights and around the corner to my stop. I stood up to leave. I turned towards our bus disc jockey who was occupied, head down once again concentrating on his machine. I have no explanation for what I did next, except that I was operating purely on impulse once again, so without thinking I moved towards him. He looked up, I offered my fisted right hand, he put down his player and accepted my salutation with his fisted right hand and we tapped knuckles. He did not seem at all surprised, perhaps he had reason to be, perhaps not. All I know is that my teenager loves telling me that I am hip, just as often as he tells me that I am not. Hip or not, down with the kids or not, at that moment, on that bus, the knuckle thing felt right. I had his attention and without thinking I said,

"Great music." He smiled, a big beaming smile, he looked happy, I walked away. Was that the end of the fun, short, yet meaningful interaction? Not quite. As I walked past the bus, something inspired me to look through the window and there he was smiling broadly perched high on his seat waiting for me to acknowledge him. So what did I do? I raised my head in one of those sharp upside down nods that my children do. Apparently I have been soaking up urban youth communication skills. Anyway, he replied with a reverse nod and that was the end of that.

A short interaction, few words and seemingly meaningless but something happened on that bus that day. Music playing on buses has a tendency to provoke a variety of responses, tempers flare, voices raise, threats issue forth, as one passenger may attempt to control the behaviour of another. Very few people enjoy being told what to do and this particular age group becomes understandably weary of persistent disapproval. They do care, they just have their own way of showing it. Perhaps my response that day made a slight difference in a small way.

*

Just for the record, I do not always dance to the enforced musical background on public transport. However, I decided a while ago that I was not going to allow it to negatively impact my mood or my day. A couple of years ago I was chatting to a guy who complained that he was having a stressful day. His view was that his tube journey was marred by the presence of not one but two (in his words) 'thoughtless teenagers' who with their music playing loudly on their headphones had (in his words) 'ruined the whole journey'.

I told him what I do in those circumstances to turn the events in my favour. I use the beat as a metronome to time my breathing and meditate along to it. I was very proud of myself for coming up with that simple solution. It happens so often, we find ourselves subjected to the possibly irritating tsk, tsk, tsk, emanating from headphones. I knew that it could be annoying but I did not want to be annoyed by it. I had to find another way to live with it. I had already learned the utter futility of expecting others to change their behaviour so that I could feel better. Now the tsk, tsk, tsk, is the basis for my travelling meditation and I feel great.

When I shared my skill with the guy in the shop he chose to still be concerned about trying to remedy (in his words) 'the thoughtlessness of others', so I wished him luck with that project and walked away.

For me, my little trick can be pleasantly entertaining for assisting with breathing in and breathing out in a controlled manner, while taking the mind away from the minutiae of everyday life which causes our stress in the first place. If I was feeling especially benevolent, I might even go as far as to say that I am thankful to the music playing person for giving me an opportunity to improve my focus. Well done me. As a bonus, this activity can prove to be joyfully meditative when combined with pelvic floor exercises. I have more than once found myself in full flow of the woven pattern of breathing, holding, squeezing and clenching, then been surprisingly disappointed when the music stops. Try it one day if you feel inspired and I challenge you not to be a teeny weeny bit grateful for the opportunity to catch up on some travelling body strengthening exercises, while you quiet your mind. Just imagine the benefits. Enough said.

*

If anyone wants to find opportunities to improve their focus on public transport then try travelling across town on a night bus, though I express caution because it is not for the faint hearted. For reasons that I do not feel inclined to go into right now, I made the odd decision to journey home from Kilburn in NW6 to Tooting in SW17 by bus at one o'clock in the morning. Without thinking I flew upstairs just like I would during the day time. My immediate impression was that I had somehow stumbled across some other world, or should I say underworld, another place of alternative human activity. Several bodies all hooded, heads down all hunched one or two mumbling here and there. It was an energy with which I was quite unfamiliar and I found it amusing.

On reflection I suppose it would have been sensible to simply about turn and place myself on the lower deck. Why did I not do that? Not sure really, I just felt that I was fine and I figured that the scattered hunched and hooded were likely to be quite unaware of my arrival anyway. I sat where I wanted to sit, upstairs by the window to enjoy the beautiful night time view of our fabulous city all lit up and gorgeous.

After a couple of minutes a person came up the stairs and plonked himself beside me. Well I think it was a he, the generic clothing, gave little away with heavy boots, baggy trousers, huge jacket and hood pulled up and over. Never mind, it did not matter because within seconds he lowered his head and leaned forward. It briefly crossed my mind that there were double seats available in front of me and behind me but he had chosen to sit beside me. Perhaps he had a particular reason, we may never know. I became unconcerned by that when in his head low and forward position, he did not look entirely comfortable. His head and upper body jerked, they jerked again, oh no... then jerked again, oh no... did I hear a muffled grunt? Was he going to ... oh no... he was going to be ...

I was trapped by the window, short of climbing over him to escape, I was wedged in. I wanted to make a hurried exit, yet it did not feel like a good idea to ask him to move, he was giving me the distinct impression that he was on the verge of revisiting the contents of his alimentary tract and while I did not want him to decorate my shoes, I did not want him to move either. I chose to follow my guidance, I chose to focus, I chose to repeatedly remind myself that he would be fine and that I would be fine.

As if responding to my inner dialogue, my hooded, jerking, grunting companion suddenly stood up and practically ran down the stairs. He obviously made it out of the door in time because I did not hear anything to the contrary. I suspect he did not get far though, however I chose not to look out of the window for evidence of his progress. I was just thankful that my shoes were safe.

*

Well that was a little night time travel. Afternoons on a bus can be pretty entertaining too particularly if the route serves a variety of secondary schools, as I have come to discover. I have a great deal of fun listening to conversations and I often find myself admiring their frank observations of this world around us. There is no question of eavesdropping or overhearing private discussions because our small or large groups of uniformed students do not seem to be concerned about the rest of the passengers hearing their shared thoughts.

I have boarded buses packed with school children at chucking out time and while they are invariably lively and chatty, I have found them to be polite and courteous. I happily witness similar behaviour from private and state school pupils and I have a selection of both to enjoy during my local journeys. I am no longer surprised when I squeeze through a mass of bodies downstairs to make my way to the top deck where I invariably find a seat. I know from observation how particular members of our younger generation can be about whoever they sit next to or indeed who they feel comfortable about sitting beside them. Therefore, I take it as a huge compliment when a child of any age but particularly a teenager sits beside me on a bus. Oh yes, I mean when they sit properly, not in that perched on the edge facing the aisle kind of sitting. No I mean sitting beside me comfortably with ease. Yes, this is a compliment. They are particular and protective about their personal space. They are also intuitive about energy yet are understandably less clear about how to express it with so many influences attempting to redirect or control their thoughts and behaviour.

I am reminded of a young girl I saw at a bus stop in Clapham Junction. In her uber smart private school uniform she appeared anxious, button pressing on her white mobile phone. It looked like a Blackberry to me but as I have said before, I do not claim to be an expert. There was a seat available but she did not sit down, she seemed to be pacing and tutting, so when she glanced in my direction, I smiled. Her furrowed brow and anxious expression implied that she was a long way from smiling back but that was okay. I had done my bit. I did not need her to respond in the same way. She clearly had things on her mind. Her response was to say,

"Do you know when the bus is coming?" Well of course I did not, no one does, this is London, the buses come when they are ready. I gave up with bus timetables a long time ago, not that I ever really bothered with them much, except perhaps to have a rough idea of the first and last bus on a route. Otherwise the timetable is meaningless. It can display a schedule of seven minute intervals, yet three will come at once. I find it easier just to release all concern about it.

Of course it is a completely different story in other communities. When we enjoyed a fabulous family holiday touring the picturesque North Yorkshire Moors by bus for two weeks, the locals openly expressed their disbelief that we had no car. Yes we did own one, yes we had left it at home, no we were not crazy, yes we were moving from town to town by bus. Anyway, there were occasions when our route was inevitably tailored to suit the bus schedule because there was just one bus that day. Yes, one a day! With two small children it was fun, they knew no different. Rain or shine, muddy or dry they loved it. For us adults it was an adventure, we knew the difference. Come rain or shine, muddy or dry we loved it.

By the way, we enjoyed a similar bus based touring holiday in Cornwall too. It was brilliant. Why so brilliant? Perhaps simply the joy of a stress free vacation without driving, searching, parking and oh so little luggage as a by-product of travelling by public transport. Anyway my point is that in this environment, there is actually an answer if someone asks the question, "Do you know when the bus is coming?"

When the young secondary school lady asked me, I said what I felt inspired to say,

"It will be here soon." Looking around in despair she let out a big moan and said,

"Oh why is it taking so long?" I did not think that she would appreciate my views on the illusion that is time, so even though she had asked the question, I accepted that it was rhetorical and kept my thoughts to myself. However, I did wonder how one so young could appear so troubled. Then her phone rang,

"Oh hi mum ..." Her conversation continued in another European language and clearly went no way, I repeat clearly went no way to easing her anxiety. She ended her conversation, paced up and down, returned and looked at me. She opened the dialogue with,

"I am supposed to be going to the theatre and if I'm late it will be a problem."

I said, "The bus will be here soon, you'll be fine."

She continued, "I have to get changed and eat as well."

I repeated, "You'll be fine." She still looked troubled and she paused from her former pacing to look at me. I knew it was really none of my business but I followed the impulse to say, "It is a lot to do after you've been at school all day, to go the theatre as well isn't it?" Her sigh came from the heart as she added,

"Yes I know and I don't like the homework, there is a lot of homework."

Her sad eyes made me say, "It sounds like it's a bit much."

She quickly confirmed, "It is a bit much."

My instinct was to offer a suggestion, "Tell your mother it's too much."

She looked at me and seemed to glaze over, perhaps as if I had suggested something utterly ridiculous or perhaps she was simply considering the scenario.

In front of me stood a young girl on the boundary of her teenage years, either approaching them or recently arrived. We were in the second week of September, so she had not been back at school for a full week yet. Considering that she had also taken at least six weeks (probably more) to recuperate during the summer break, I wondered how it was possible for her to be feeling overwhelmed by her school life. She was overwhelmed enough to share her anxiety with a complete stranger. Poor child, what was going on? Why was she already on a treadmill? There are quite enough adults choosing a fast pace of daily living, without realising the slow pattern of self-destruction. It does not feel good, it is unsustainable and the results become evident.

Moving on.

*

I boarded a single decker on a Wednesday evening and after greeting the driver I quickly scanned the seating availability and noticed a little movement from a couple of bodies on the back seat. I particularly remember it was a Wednesday because I particularly remember where I had been but more about that later. The back seat was occupied, then the next three pairs of seats on both sides were all vacant and several people sat at the front section of the bus. Like I say, it was a quick scan so I did not give myself time to wonder why there was a huge gap instead of people being spread out like normal. Never mind, I walked to the back and sat by the window on the left, in front of the very back row. All was quiet. I was comfortable. I was happy. I felt fine. Then it began…

A male voice began to speak then a female voice joined in. At first I thought they were talking to each other but soon realised that they were the comedy act for the journey. I do not claim to know the source of their inspiration but I soon witnessed their entertainment style. The two voices came from behind me and took it in turns to single out passengers on the bus for a running commentary, describing their clothes, hair, appearance, face and expressions. Not satisfied with their focus on people's physical aspects the two voices tried their psychic skills by guessing what people were thinking, where they were going, where they had come from, and what they did for a living. When I say 'describing' and 'guessing' I shall also add that nothing I heard sounded complimentary.

What was their intention? I had no idea. I was sitting immediately in front of them and while I had not looked at them closely, from my peripheral vision I saw that the guy sat by the window on my right with his legs on the seat and directly behind me sat the girl by the window with her legs up on the seat facing her partner in their double act. So there was me sitting in front of them, with all those empty seats in front of me and everyone else sitting right at the front of the bus. When their talking began, I understood why there was such a gap and have no doubt that they had started before I boarded, so the seating arrangement made absolute sense.

Well this was an interesting situation. Passengers were being identified, singled out and spoken about with little mercy being shown. I was not unduly bothered and I can only assume that was due to feeling good about myself and not paying any attention to what anyone else thinks about me. If this couple chose to be pleasant or unpleasant it was no concern of mine, I could choose to love them anyway, knowing that whatever they pretended, they were just like the rest of us wanting to love and be loved, even if they were not consciously aware of it.

So while their performance was going on, I looked out of the window finding things to appreciate, when it occurred to me that they had passed comment on every passenger on the vehicle, every person except me. Geographically I was the first in the line of fire, as I was immediately in front of them. How odd then that they diverted their attention from one person to another, returning to some for a second and third dose, without including me in the mix. How odd indeed. It was almost as if they could not see me. Interesting. I thought about the situation and smiled to myself with some measure of understanding.

Several minutes passed by (well minutes for me, probably an eternity for others) then from the girl behind me I heard,

"Ooh, look a hula hoop." Her friend immediately laughed and said,

"Oh yeah, I like hula hooping, it's great exercise." Well imagine my surprise when they suddenly started talking about this fantastic hobby. Oh did I forget to mention that I was the one with the hula hoop? Yes it was me, I had boarded the bus with a forty inch hoop, alright, a hundred and two centimetres for you metric readers. It was not insignificantly decorated in red glitter, pink shiny and white matt tape. I am not talking about a foldaway version in a case that may be easy to miss, no I mean a fully open, circular, waist high, get in the way, hard to hide, impossible to ignore kind of hoop. Having my hoop as luggage was one of the reasons I was glad of the space to sit at the back of the bus when it arrived. It was beside me encroaching on the aisle, so … there was simply no way that the rear seat comedy duo could have missed it. So how on earth did they not seem to notice it or me before? Interesting.

The female added, "Yeah, it's really hard though but it's fun." It was then that I decided to ignore their previous behaviour and turn around. I looked at the boy first and smiled, he smiled back, I continued slowly turning, I was totally unprepared for what I was to see. We made eye contact, we smiled and I was stunned. I found myself looking at the face of an angel, she was absolutely beautiful. For some reason I was surprised by her beauty. Was this the same face, with the same mouth, out of which came the words I had heard earlier? I just remember looking at her and feeling utterly convinced that I was beholding the face of a divine being. I smiled at her for longer than was necessary and I suppose some may say for longer than advisable given their earlier conduct. I did not think about that, I did not care, I was at that moment looking at peace and serenity.

I said, "Yes it is fun" and turned away to face forward again.

Some might say coincidence but from that moment everyone else on the bus was off the hook. The back seat conspirators considerably lowered their voices and talked to each other about their friendships, relationships, parents, school, going out and staying in. The dynamics on the bus were entirely transformed and the sequence of events on that journey, continue to intrigue me. Several minutes later, my stop was fast approaching so I rose to leave with my hoop toy. The beautiful young girl looked at me brightly and said,

"Have fun with your hula hoop," I thanked her then the boy said,

"Say a prayer for me." What? Where did that come from? I had no idea then and I have no idea now why he said that, all I know is that all was well. He said it with a happy, peaceful, smiling, calm expression.

It was an intriguing sequence of events and while I may not be able to explain it, I know that something happened on that bus that day between me and those two young adults.

*

So I said earlier that I remember it was a Wednesday because of where I had been. Well, I was on my way home from a hooping class, held in a church hall in Clapham. I had really enjoyed myself and I feel inspired to say that it is hard not to enjoy myself when hooping. It is a new activity for me and I am pleasantly surprised by the joy it brings. I can lose myself in the sensation of the hoop and it feels quite meditative. Perhaps more about that in another publication, if I feel so inspired, anyway for now my hoop has been instrumental in prompting brief encounters with strangers and I do not mean at classes or gatherings of other like-minded hoop lovers.

I shall allow myself the indulgence of straying from bus related encounters for a moment. I guess this is my book so I can really do what I like. This is so much more fun than writing on forums or contributing to newsletters. I never enjoyed the irritation of someone else changing my thoughts and words. This is the answer, to write my own book, yay!

I walked along Franciscan Road in Tooting one sunny afternoon and an old lady stopped me in the street to ask me if the hoop I was carrying belonged to me or whether I had bought it for someone else. She seemed to have a lot of fun telling me how she used to hoop when she was a girl and how that was a long time ago and how she is too old to do it now and how she was happy to see me with one and how they are not just for children and

Carole Chandler

how they are great exercise. She seemed quite sprightly for her seventy seven years of age, yet I imagine she probably could give it another go if the fancied the idea.

A little further along the same road on the same day, I have no idea why, perhaps it was the weather, a little old man ran out of a shop to tell me that he saw me coming with the hoop and wanted to ask if it was mine and whether I knew how to use it. How interesting, he really surprised me with his excited questioning.

Around the corner on the same day I turned into a main road and a lady pushing a buggy walked beside me and asked if I had bought the hoop for someone else. When I told her it was for me, she wanted to know more, particularly as she had heard it was good exercise and considered it for helping to regain her pre pregnancy figure.

Another day, another hoop, I was in a fabric shop in Merton High Street near Wimbledon, I browsed with my hoop over my shoulder when a young couple came in and we found ourselves chatting in the rear corner of the shop. The girl said that she enjoyed hula hooping and given her neat trim little figure, bright expression, bubbly personality and sports clothing, I wondered if she was a teacher in the fine craft of hoop dancing. For some reason my question made her laugh. I have no idea why because she could easily have been a teacher and I was not to know that she had just started to learn hooping skills herself.

Never mind, she found it funny and that is okay. Her boyfriend just smiled as we spoke and I said something about him being patient while we nattered away. It was then my turn to laugh when she said that he was more likely to be better at hooping than her. Well he did look as though he had been eyeing it up during our chat, so I offered it to him. With all of us laughing, he took it then returned it, when it dawned on us that there was not nearly enough room in a shop full of bolts of fabrics and carousels of buttons and shelves of ribbons, for the spinning and turning and flipping and whirling of a large rubber tube. Not just any tube but a circular tube which uncannily develops a mind of its own, as the contents of my lounge could testify. We chatted more about fun in the hoop and parted cheerfully. I do not remember if any of us actually bought anything but the shop peeps did not seem to object to us merry making in their store.

I met a delightful lady on a jive dance holiday in Devon who entertained us at dinner with stories about how she had recently discovered a love of hooping and immediately enjoyed a change in her body shape as a result. Her age is probably irrelevant but I just feel like adding that she was sharing her interest with her teenage grand-daughter. Perhaps that may be enough to persuade others to give it a try and not allow age to be a barrier.

Then there was the time I left my hoop class on another Wednesday evening in Clapham. I had a different hoop with me, this one a little smaller, thirty seven inches, which may not sound much to the uninitiated but makes a huge difference in the learning process and calls upon different technical challenges. Anyway this one taped in black and pink was yet again impossible to ignore, they can be a little unwieldy and I was grateful for the especially wide pavement opposite Clapham Common and indeed the paths on the common itself to avoid wiping out people as I made my way to the bus stop.

My life experiences have taught me that everything is meant to be. Sometimes I find myself in places, wondering why I am there and then just waiting to see what transpires. This was one such occasion. I sat at the bus stop and found myself in easy conversation with a delightful lady, so nothing so unusual about that. I managed to prop my hoop behind the bench and I am not sure that she even saw it. She had a delicious Irish accent and I enjoyed listening to her speaking. Allow me to take a moment to give a big shout to anyone who has already enjoyed my first book about strangers in Ireland, where I mention once or twice my love affair with the Irish musical speaking voices.

It was nice to hear her voice and I loved hearing how she likes living in London and that she took a while to settle after leaving Ireland but she feels really at home now. She had a lovely easy way of conversing, so much so, that it was a while before I realised that a bus had not arrived in all the time we were there. Someone came along and checked the timetable and asked if the one which was 'due' had been seen. That was when my companion said (surprisingly without the slightest hint of irritation) that she had been waiting for an hour. Really! What about me? I do not wear a watch, so I had not realised that she and I had been chatting for forty minutes. I learned this from her because seemingly, she had checked the time when I arrived, just out of curiosity. Why was she so content to sit and wait for a bus which, even from my perspective, was a long time coming. She explained that she walked with the aid of a stick, due to her mobility issues and she had shopping bags, so it was worth her while to sit and wait because the bus stops outside her front door. I made a suggestion, what about a cab? I would be happy to hail one for her but she was not interested, naming cost as an issue.

Well by then I had convinced myself that no matter how much I was enjoying her company, my guidance was to follow my own suggestion and enjoy a cab ride home. I said goodbye and walked thirty seconds to a busy corner, along came a cab and I was on my way.

Now then, anyone who is familiar with London cabbies knows how they love to talk. I have resisted the temptation to tell tales of chats with cab drivers in my last book because there is nothing unusual about that. The general experience is that they will talk to anyone about anything, just ask the inimitable Peter Kay. However, I do feel compelled to share a pretty unusual experience which my wonderful son enjoyed. He has somehow developed a gift of being able to talk to a variety of people on a variety of subjects and sometimes surprises me with the stories he tells about his own travels. I wonder where he has inherited that from? He was in a London taxi cab negotiating the streets of the centre of our capital city, making slow progress, enjoying a lively dialogue with the driver, who was having such fun with their conversation that he, wait for it … turned off his meter! I was gobsmacked when he told me. In all my born days I have never heard of a London taxi driver turning off his meter before. Wow, he must have been having a really good time. Time is money right? The driver essentially gave my son a gift. It was not my experience so why did I feel equally blessed when he told me? I have no idea but I nearly cried. It was a wonderful blessing bestowed on one of my nearest and dearest. A blessing indeed and something to appreciate, something to be grateful for, or I could say, something for which to be grateful, if I am to be grammatically accurate. Never mind, as I have said before, apart from the pedants among us, who actually speaks like that?

So back to my Wednesday evening, hoop carrying, tired of bus waiting, cab riding encounter. The driver asked if I was having a good evening and I told him about my fun hoop class. My life experience had already taught me not to bother with the whole bus not arriving scenario and just focus on the happy stuff. He seemed interested, so I chatted excitedly about how much fun the hooping activity can be. He seemed to think that I had learned some time ago, that I had been doing it for a while and might even be quite proficient. I assured him that they were all far from the truth. I was new, brand new and taking my first formal course of classes instead of relying on the internet for my tutorials. Even though they are excellent for demonstrating new skills, there is something additionally beneficial about sharing the fun and frustrations of repeatedly hooping and dropping, with other newbies. How can it still be so much fun to do something which you are rubbish at? It just is.

I suppose it was something about my enthusiasm for learning something new that encouraged the driver to tell me that he had always wanted to learn to play the guitar. Of course I asked,

"So what is stopping you?" He said something about being too old. Well I was not about to let him get away with so feeble an excuse. Surely he has heard of other adults learning new skills? He was keen but did not know where to begin or how to read music and did not fancy the idea of learning in a group with children. Again, I was not prepared to settle for those excuses.

I told him about when I learned to read music by learning to play the flute after my son was born. I was an adult starting from scratch and I did not know a quaver from a semibreve. It was a steep learning curve but I progressed through theory and practical exams, to playing grade eight pieces for fun. I told him about the option of private lessons, to learn at his own pace, taking his own sweet time. I took it upon myself to say that there was nothing to stop him, just buy an instrument, find a teacher, make no more excuses and do something which has always interested him. I enjoyed seeing his sweet face brighten up with a big beaming smile in his rear view mirror. I was flattered when he said that our conversation had inspired him and he had there and then made the decision to "just do it".

So when I was home (eventually) I wondered about my long bus stop interlude with the Irish lady and my sudden decision to catch a taxi and my 'chance' meeting with the cabbie, considering that my arrival around the corner a few seconds earlier or later, we would have never met. For all I know he is now playing a guitar joyfully on a regular basis, reaping the rewards of such a stress reducing, character building, self-esteem raising hobby. How wonderful it would be if he had improved his life experience as a result of our little chat? I would be happy to say, "You're welcome".

Just for funzies, let me tell you what inspired me to learn to play the flute. I took my daughter to a performance of 'The Ugly Duckling' at the Polka Theatre, the wonderful children's theatre in Wimbledon, when she was a wee little thing, probably about three or four years old. One of the performers played a variety of flutes in the show when the divine melodic sounds simply sang to me and I was smitten. I bought an instrument, found a teacher and I allowed myself to grow musically.

*

So returning to the world of adults and bus journeys, one day I waited at a stop on the Mitcham Road for my wonderful majestic red machine and equally wonderful majestic driver to take me home. The bus shelter had a long red seat and I chose to put my bag at one end and I stood beside it. I felt no particular inclination to be seated as the bus was expected soon and I was far from tired. An elderly lady arrived, shuffling with a walking stick, a full plastic bag and a grumpy attitude. She was welcome to all of them and I smiled at her anyway, as she sat down with some difficulty at the far end of the seat. During the next few minutes she maintained a persistent state of agitation, checking the LED indicator and the approaching vehicles at ten second intervals, interspersing her observations with tuts, grunts, moans and voiced complaints about her dissatisfaction with the timing of her transport's arrival. I had no intention of interrupting her negativity. There were many things I could have said but I thought better of it. She had not reached her current perspective overnight so she would be unlikely to entertain my way of thinking and if she did hear me, she may have been inclined to find my words irritating if not worse. I kept my thoughts to myself and remembered that for her, as with everyone, all is well.

A man of noticeably unsteady gait approached the bus shelter, he stood in front of the long seat for a moment and instead of sitting in the middle, where there was plenty of room, he sat beside my bag, right beside my bag, close enough that his body was touching it. I was not bothered. I felt no impulse to relocate my luggage or myself, so we both remained in situ. As he took his place, the lady at the other end of the seat looked at our new arrival, grunted, stood up with some difficulty, took a few steps away from us and stood in the middle of the pavement, where she observed and scowled from her new vantage point.

I was interested because this old lady with the stick, not only carried her bag with whatever was in it, she also carried a considerable amount of extra weight and her movements were visibly impaired. I figured that her decision to vacate her seat must have been triggered by something significant. From where she stood, she glared in our direction and she did not look comfortable. Never mind, I was not to know her thought process, so I left her to it.

Meanwhile, the unsteady man and my bag were both perched at the extreme end of an otherwise empty bench. He seemed content to sit and stare forward, not at anything in particular and he paid no attention to the bus arrival indicator, so his need for a bus appeared to be not as keen as ours. After a couple of minutes his head turned slowly, very slowly, deliberately, quite deliberately to his right, in my direction, he faced me, he looked up at me. I looked down at his face and met his wild staring eyes fixed upon my face. When I say fixed, I am not altogether convinced that the wild staring eyes could see me or if they were at that moment able to focus on me or anything really. I do not claim to be an expert on the human alteration of physical features affected by light in outside spaces but the whites of his eyes had been replaced by a glorious shade of red. Well, it would have been a glorious shade indeed, were it not for the fact that it was in a place where an equally glorious shade of white is more commonly found. I try not to be surprised or caught off guard and the phrase, *'expect the unexpected'* springs to mind. Why do I say that? Who knows?

The man's eyes looked at me with a fixed stare. I looked at him. I consciously and deliberately softened my gaze and made the decision to look at him for a moment longer. His eyes looked empty, like there was nothing there but there must have been something there somewhere, of course there must have been. I knew that the greatest gift I had to offer him at that moment was to see him in the fullness of who he really is, whether he was aware of it or not. Any of us can do that in a heartbeat, I chose to find that thought there and then. I offered a smile, a small smile, a gentle smile, anything more did not feel appropriate. His expression remained unchanged. When I decided that our non-verbal communication required at least a pause, I looked away. In response, so did he.

Not one of us moved, the lady, the man, my bag and me, all remained just as we were. About a minute later, he slowly, very slowly started to turn his head towards me again and the whole eye contact, word free scenario repeated itself. When complete he seemed somehow satisfied and without a syllable uttered from either of us, he stood up and slowly, unsteadily walked away.

Moments later, the lady grunted and retraced her steps back to her position on the seat, where she resumed her erstwhile checking, observing, tutting, grunting and moaning. I do not need to be an expert in everything but I am an expert witness and can always be secure in my view of events from my perspective. Everyone has their own view, their unique perspective and their individual opinion. Of course they do, that is how the world works, that is precisely how life is supposed to be. Something happened between the three of us at that bus stop on that day. Something happened on a variety of levels and we each played our own part.

*

Something else happened on a bus a little while ago which reminded me about observations of and reactions to events around us. On my way to a tango lesson in central London, I was sitting upstairs of a 155 just leaving the shopping high street of our vibrant Brixton, when there was a change in the calm of our journey. The driver hit the brakes, the bus hit the kerb and there was a shriek from outside, followed closely by a collection of shrieks inside. This was immediately accompanied by a mass mobilisation of people from the back of the bus to the front.

Where were they all going? Why did they all jump up at once? Why the joint decision to all do the same thing? Why the impulse to move at the same time? I was momentarily baffled but not really interested enough to ask anyone. I did not even feel the inclination to, well, to do anything really. I sat in my seat while the gathering jostled each other at the front for a view out of the window at whatever it was they wanted a view of. A few people ran downstairs, they were followed by a couple more. One or two returned to report to the front window assembled company.

I sat, I waited, I assumed that at some point in the not too distant future, a management decision would be made and we would either move on or all be asked to leave. It was the latter. I walked downstairs leaving several people still unsettled running backwards and forwards on both decks of the vehicle discussing the recent events.

For the inquisitive among you, it transpired that an unattended canine member of the community had mistimed his road crossing, been clipped by the bus, yelped and ran off. The word on the street was that he was fine. The driver however was not and intended to drive no further. We were instructed to await the arrival of the next bus.

My interest, if I had any, was more in the mass frenzy. There was a frenetic excitement following our sudden stop, an excitement not dissimilar to a party or riot atmosphere, sometimes it can be hard to tell the difference. From my observations no one actually did anything constructive, they simply wound themselves into a collective tizzy. I was not derailed emotionally by the event because I have learned to *'expect the unexpected'*. Why do I say that? Who knows?

A few months later I was on my way to the Tate Modern, minding my own business upstairs by the window of a number 77. Just approaching Wandsworth Road station, we experienced a similar scenario. The driver hit the brakes, the bus hit the kerb, minus the shriek outside, I found myself once again a silent, stationary witness to a collection of shrieks inside our vehicle and another mass mobilisation of people to the front window. There was that joint activity thing again. I felt no guidance to join them, I felt no inspiration to leave my seat, I felt no indication to scream and run back and forth unconstructively.

Before the unexplained commotion a young lady had been sitting peacefully behind me. She too ran to the front with everyone else and during the continued movement I saw her looking at me. Perhaps inspired by my inactivity, she returned to her seat. The back, forth, upstairs, downstairs, frenzy continued, while she sat behind me and I continued to feel happy right where I was. As before, I awaited the inevitable vehicle movement or instruction to leave. It was the latter. On our way down the stairs the young lady was close behind me, she asked if I knew what had happened. I stopped, turned, looked, smiled and said slowly,

"I have no idea. Everything will be fine." She looked a little confused but smiled back.

A crowd of people collected on the pavement right outside the bus door, waving arms, raising voices, analysing the whys and wherefores of the abrupt cessation of our journey. I gently eased my way through them and walked ahead to the next bus stop. I was amused to see the young lady a couple of paces behind me. We were the only ones to leave the mass frenzy behind, to do whatever it is that the mass frenzy does when it has wound itself into a collective tizzy.

For the inquisitive among you, it transpired that no people or animals were involved in what someone later called 'the accident'. Seemingly, we had at slow speed connected with an item of street furniture and the driver made the decision to drive no further.

Once again my interest, if I had any, was in the response of the human collective. Interesting. Interesting indeed. Thankfully the previous two events which I have described have not repeated themselves and all is well.

*

The closest I have come to these experiences was one day on a Sunday on another 77 this time moving nicely up Earslfield Road, when we stopped at St Ann's Hill. For some reason the rear door decided it was going to pretend to close, then spring itself back open again. It did the same thing again, then again and again. I was sitting downstairs, which was out of character for me come to think of it. I wonder why I had chosen to do that? Just an impulse in the moment I suppose. The doors played their close half way and spring open game and I was treated to responses from other passengers. It was quite amusing really. Not once but twice, a man shouted "Oh come on!" He turned in his seat looking towards the driver in disgust. A lady at the front took it upon herself to approach the driver and instruct him to "get a move on". How funny. It was not as if he was purposely keeping us there, with a dodgy door on a stationary vehicle. He was probably the one person on the entire vehicle who was most desirous of being on our way. I guessed that he did not really want a mutiny on his hands. From his cockpit position he tried and tried and but to no avail.

A lady beside me shouted, "Oh no, the bus is broken!" Really? Why, 'oh no'? She looked at me and I sincerely hoped that she had no intention of including me in a guessing game about whether the vehicle was indeed broken or not. I was content to entertain myself with the idea that the door was having a Disney moment and while feeling a bit moody had simply decided to take on a character of its own. After several attempts from the front, the driver left his seat, walked back to the iffy doors, gave them a tug, a push, a pull and a kick, then hey presto, all was well.

*

On reflection, one of the things that could have been responsible for the door distraction was perhaps something stuck in the mechanism. I suspect that could easily happen with hundreds of people passing through every day. Is it hundreds or is it thousands? It is certainly a lot anyway. Perhaps there was some food stuck in the way, preventing the door from closing properly. Perhaps it was a chicken bone, perhaps a banana skin, perhaps a handful of orange peel or perhaps an apple core. This book is about my experiences, these tales are specific to me, so I can say that when I lived in Richmond, admittedly I did not move about my public transport on a daily basis like I do now, yet it must have been a fair number of times in the twenty years I had of enjoying journeys on the local 33 or 337. In all that time I do not recall seeing the remnants of lunch and dinner decorating the deck. So what is it about where I live now? Fruit peelings in abundance, oranges seem to be a popular choice, chicken bones a plenty, protein in the form of poultry flesh seems to be a particular favourite. I have noticed that the most popular seat position for discarded food is at the very front, although to be fair, I never sit right at the back. Anyway, many a time I have excitedly moved towards the prime front seat position for the fun of an unobstructed view along my way, only to find a collection of the aforementioned food items strewn across the floor. Hey, at least they are generally on the floor and not accessorising the seat. See what I mean, there is always something to be grateful for, it is always about perspective.

*

That is quite enough about food on the floor, so instead I shall relive a food inspired interaction which amused me a little while ago. I found myself at Amen Corner on the edge of Tooting waiting for a 57 or 333 to my favourite café in Streatham. It is not a bus stop which I use regularly, in fact I think I have only ever used it once before and not since the time I am about to share. I had just arrived at the shelter and was happily standing alone until a lady walked quickly to join me.

She put her bag of groceries on the seat and started rummaging. Of course when she looked at me I smiled, of course I did, why would I not? She continued fussing, taking things out of her bag and putting things back. She produced another bag from somewhere as if by magic and I wondered if a rabbit might appear any moment soon.

Instead of allowing the entertainment to keep me distracted, she handed me a bag and asked if I would help her rearrange her shopping. Naturally, I was happy to help but I still think it was an unusual situation to find myself in. This lady just asked a total stranger to be instrumental in her impromptu organisational activities at a bus stop. I do not think for a moment that this is an everyday event. Well I have never witnessed this before. Perhaps it is just me, perhaps it is just my life but I found it really funny to be included in her rummaging.

*

Part of my inspiration for writing this book is to share stories about just how lovely and nice and kind and friendly unknown people can be. Anyone, indeed everyone can talk about the unpleasantness of bus travel and I am quite aware that it happens.

Soon after I moved to this London post code I found myself one evening in rush hour at the bus stop outside a Wandsworth council office. It is this combination of factors which jointly contribute towards my motivation to ensure, that I do not repeat the experience. Even from my 'everything is alright' and 'all is well' and 'think positive' place of observation, it is still up to me to choose where I wish to be. I have a dear friend, who once wisely reminded me that with utter faith and belief in our well-being, we could stand in the middle of the M25 and be fine but it does not mean we will choose to do it.

Some places at certain times of the day are just so packed with people that our five physical senses are simply overwhelmed. On this day, a crowd of about a hundred million people were gathered on the pavement. I leave you to decide on the extent of my exaggeration. I make no excuse other than to stress that there were a lot of people, such a lot of people. A bus came and its approach induced a significant amount of activity. I had no desire to be in the centre of the throng but I did have a desire to be on my way home. I suspect a number of people were of similar intent. The bus stopped, the door opened and the huddle moved as one. Again I would just like to say that I was quite content to be on the periphery. Every experience is a learning experience and what I next witnessed taught me something.

People started to board and while it was busy, the movement seemed absent of pushing or jostling. Perhaps that was simply another one of those perspective things. All movement suddenly stopped when a woman at the entrance of the bus, turned to the woman next to her and yelled,

"You touch my arm again and I'll knock you out!" That was it. No swearing, no fisticuffs, just a clear sentence, a distinct statement of desire and declaration of intent. The thing I remember was that not one person batted an eyelid. I saw no reaction from anyone. I felt unable to assume anything other than we were witnessing normal behaviour. I am loath to believe that it was seen as acceptable behaviour but perhaps unsurprising. Well, I was surprised. I was new to the area. I have learned more about myself, as the last few years have gone by and improving my understanding of others has proven to be a welcome by product.

*

Thankfully that little scene did not become a familiar event. To be honest I have never seen anything like it, so if lucky is the word then lucky is what I am. I read a poster not long ago, informing us of the intention of one of our glorious political leaders in charge of transport, wishing to clamp down on antisocial behaviour on buses. I do not see it. If it exists then it must be that I do not rendezvous with it. Then again …

I was at the Wimbledon road bus stop on Garratt Lane when a double decker pulled up short of the shelter. The rear doors opened, several people piled out. There was a pause. The lights on the bus went out. Interesting. The engine stopped running. Interesting. There were people on board. Interesting. The front door opened. I heard shouting from a woman standing by the door. The driver shouted, she shouted back, the driver said,

"What is it about the word NO that you don't understand?" Ouch! I was eternally grateful not to know what that was all about and I decided that there was no way I would be travelling anywhere on that vehicle, with evidence of at least two less than joyous people on board. I walked away from them. I could wait for the next. I did not mind waiting. I had no desire to discover what the passengers and their driver were leading up to. The opportunities for negative experiences were ever increasing with a grumpy driver whatever ever his reason, no matter how valid it may seem. From my place of joy, love and peace I would probably be fine whatever the circumstances but why risk it?

*

Another day I was at the same bus stop on my way to Covent Garden for some fun time of pretending I live there again. A bus arrived, the front door opened and there were so many people downstairs that I would have had to squeeze past to get on. Ordinarily that does not bother me, as often I have found a seat available upstairs even with many standing downstairs. However, I have learned to follow my guidance or call it instinct, or impulse or urge or intuition.

We give the same gut feeling a lot of different names but the result is always the same, if we follow it we are on the right track and if we do not follow it, then ... Well, you know what happens when you do something that does not feel right. We all have this feeling. It seems that for many people the hurdle is learning to trust that this feeling is always right, always, without exception. Learning to trust our inner guidance is the most accurate indication we have at our disposal. It is utterly consistent and we have it forever.

So I stood at the door, glanced at the bodies and signalled to the driver that I had changed my mind. He drove off. A chap beside me on the pavement took my reverse decision as his cue to share his opinions about our bus service in general. He had plenty to say about his perceived lack of vehicles, the inadequacies of drivers, the tardiness of arrivals, the failures of politicians and oh so much more. I do not know what he wanted from me, I could not join him because I did not agree and I did not care enough to argue with him. I felt no compulsion to offer my feelings of appreciation for our buses in this wonderful city because he expressed such an opposing view.

Anyway, I had let the bus go and as we were near the beginning of the route, I expected to be there for the scheduled twelve minutes, before the arrival of the next. By way of passing the time, I began to look around for things to enjoy when lo and behold around the corner came a bus after a couple of minutes. Yay, I was saved from hearing more from my complaining bus stop companion.

I sat upstairs on a peaceful vehicle and prepared to enjoy my trip. Three stops later the previous bus had come to a halt, everyone from it was out in the cold waiting to join ours. How interesting. How wonderful that I had saved myself the bother of squeezing and standing on the first busy one, followed by the irritation of relocating. Interesting. How nice to have evidence once again that there is benefit in following my guidance. I appreciate that this example seems relatively insignificant but it is simply one of my many excuses for knowing why I think the way I do.

*

Woah, stop press, hold everything I simply must share. Blessed as I am with the daily pleasure of chatting to strangers, a couple of days ago I received a gift, of the most wonderful interaction, which gave me more pleasure that I could have imagined.

It was a Saturday afternoon and I had just paid a visit to my favourite art shop on the Mitcham Road to treat myself to a few supplies for my meditation inspired artistic creations. The bus stop is conveniently just a few metres away so I walked out of the door and turned left. I saw a beautiful Route Master by the bus stop. Well that alone was pretty unusual because in our current age of modern transport, the humble Route Masters now spend their retirement years providing tourists with photographic opportunities on the number 15 for the Tower of London and the number 9 for The Royal Albert Hall. Both of these routes are in the centre of London not in the south west suburbs.

I saw that it said Wedding Special on the back and assumed that it was passing through, waiting in traffic on its way through the area to another destination. As I reached the stop, I was surprised to see that it had not paused in traffic but had stopped. It was parked, there at the bus stop. Well where else would it park? It was a bus after all. Not only that, to my amazement there was another Route Master wedding special parked in front of it. It was lovely to see them, my children remember travelling on them and now I feel a hint of nostalgia wafting over me. Route Masters are so much fun and promote a strange sense of freedom, taking your chances, choosing your moment to jump on and off, in traffic away from the kerb. They disappeared for a while but have now been reintroduced on the circuit and a modernised version can be found on the number 38 route out of Victoria.

Hold on a moment if we are talking about nostalgia then a conversation I overheard on my coach to Bristol last week was just the ticket. (Do you see what I did there, just the ticket, buses, coaches ...) The driver had a lively conversation with a lady sitting in the front seat as they both talked about the old days and I had fun listening to them. He said that he has been driving coaches for thirty years and was a bus driver before that. They reminisced about the old buses and the demise of the conductor element of public transport journeys. Apparently when 'they' decided to do away with conductors, 'they' could not make them redundant so 'clippies' became the first female bus drivers. Well that was interesting to know, I learned something new. I tried not to laugh when he said that some of them were good at driving buses even though they were women. He was talking to a woman at the time and she let him get away with it too, so I followed suit. Enough about them, time to return my attention to the Tooting wedding bus.

I sat at the bus shelter and enjoyed the wonderful sight of beautiful people drifting off their majestic vehicles and congregating on the pavement all around me. They were nothing to do with me but I simply basked in their excitement. A delightful collection of handsome young men all nicely suited, along with beautiful young ladies gorgeously dressed in a glorious array of colours and prints and flowers and lace. I also saw some the highest heels I have seen for a long time. All credit to the lady in the sapphire blue, suede, peep toe, vertiginous creations which really caught my eye.

I could not help smiling at the joyous scene. Several of them smiled back, even the gentlemen struggling with a crate of champagne and ice, somehow found the space to return my smile. The atmosphere was so much fun that I was in danger of sitting there with the sole intention of observing the spectacle, instead of watching out for my bus home.

Now then do not get me wrong, I love to see a wedding but I am not one of those sad ladies who hangs around outside churches waiting to see the happy couple. For the pedants among my readers, when I say 'hangs around', I do not mean in the literal sense like a bat or a line of washing, of course I merely say 'hangs around' in the colloquial sense. Anyway, that is not me, not even the time I found myself at Fulham Palace waiting for the arrival of the bride. No, that time does not count. I was enjoying a lovely walk on a beautiful summer's day in Bishop's Park in Fulham, when while passing through the grounds I saw a gentleman setting up a table of glasses. Then around the corner I saw a couple of handsome young men exquisitely dressed in slate grey morning suits and royal blue cravats, looking like princes waiting at a castle gate for the arrival of an important queen. I continued walking and saw another equally handsome, exquisitely dressed chap at the other end of the driveway. I was already excited and saw no reason to pretend not to be interested, so I asked the lone driveway guardian when the bride was expected to arrive. He said that she was due any minute, so I decided to wait. I told him that seeing as the guys looked so well turned out the bride must be worth seeing.

There were a couple of ladies sitting on a nearby wall, their cute dogs seemed happy to wait patiently too, so I joined them. They told me that they knew the bride from dog walking and we all agreed that it is fun to see brides and bridesmaids. The whole spectacle of the event promised to be worth the effort and as it was a lovely afternoon, waiting there was a fun way to pass the time. We all concluded that we were in a great position because the driveway entrance was blocked by posts in the ground. That meant that whenever she arrived, the vehicle would be forced to stop, she would be forced to get out and we would be afforded the perfect view of her in her finery on her special day, as she paraded along the path to the Palace.

Well no sooner had we prided ourselves on our timing and positioning, that a killjoy came along and promptly removed the posts. Bother. That meant the car would be able to drive straight in and we were to be denied the pleasure of our visual treat. What a spoilsport. Did he not know that we were waiting to be part of the appreciation party? Did he not know that we were the self-appointed welcoming committee? I repeat, what a spoilsport. Never mind I took the change in circumstance as my cue to bid adieu to the wall sitters and their dogs and to continue my stroll around the grounds.

So where was I? Ah yes, I was in the middle of denying that I sit around waiting for weddings to happen. So there I was at the bus stop in Tooting, when a wedding party came to me. While I enjoyed observing the happy activity, a lady stood right slap bang in front of me. She looked like a divine goddess in a glorious gold gown. I was quite content to admire and appreciate her dress, convinced that it had been hand crafted in silk and taffeta by a master dressmaker. Imagine that, gold silk and taffeta with a lace, chiffon, organza type detail going on around the superbly fitting strapless bodice. Her dark brown hair curled in cute ringlets, beautifully cascading down her back, draping her shoulders creating the perfect top line for her dress. She stood before me, right in front of me, under the shelter, cool, calm and collected, contentedly standing in the cold, shivering, holding a glass of champagne and smiling. Yes shivering and smiling. I am not a fan of being cold and I would struggle to shiver and smile, even if I looked like an angel sent from heaven, like she did in her glorious, gorgeous, golden gown.

I looked at her and asked the only question which seemed appropriate in that moment,

"Are you the bride?" Well if it were possible for her to look even more beautiful, she did as she said,

"Yes I am." I congratulated her and she thanked me, I felt inspired to continue,

"Your guests look like they're having fun."

"Oh yes they are, they are very special to me and it is wonderful to have them here." I was taken by the way she said it, she sounded so sincere and I was delighted for her.

I said, "How wonderful that you are surrounded by them."

"Yes, I'm having a fabulous time," she replied.

I believed every word of it, she looked like she was indeed having a fabulous time. She was obviously a special person to have so many people who are special to her and enjoying her special day with her.

I explained that I wondered if she were the bride because she looked so calm but she simply said that her day was fun and all was going well. She asked me a question,

"Are you a local?"

"Yes indeed I am and I have never had a treat like this before at my local bus stop so thank you for being here." Between you and me I was unconsciously saying thanks to the Universe for lining me up with this joyous occasion but that is by the by. I thought it was funny that she should ask because I was observing the spectacle before me and wondering why they were there because this large group of beautiful people did not look like locals at all. As if reading my thoughts she said,

"We are holding the reception in this pub." The venue was right in front of us and they were waiting to be allowed into the function room upstairs. I remember thinking that the inside space of this unassuming exterior must be nicer than I had expected, for it to be the chosen location for the celebrations of these beautiful people. Then again, my impression was that they were in such a happy positive emotional place that they could have gathered anywhere and continued their celebrations regardless of the setting.

This lovely lady seemed content to stand shivering, still champagne holding, still smiling in front of me, willingly engaging me in conversation. I expected her to join one or more of the many members of her wedding party, instead of standing there with little me but she seemed to be in no hurry to be anywhere, other than where she was at that moment. So cool, so calm, so collected, I was impressed.

I asked, "Where did you hold the ceremony?"

"Islington Town Hall, so we've come a long way across town, it was fun on the buses in the traffic." Woah, she was not kidding, from north to south, the revellers had quite a journey to continue and maintain their excitement, by the time I stumbled across them. I was on the verge of telling her that I know where the town hall is in Islington, having spent some time socialising and visiting friends in that part of town, when we were interrupted.

A little older lady beautifully coordinated in her green dress, long jacket and lovely hat needed the attention of the golden, gowned goddess. My new friend said,

"It's alright mummy, I'm talking to this nice lady." Ooh, how sweet was that? Her mother looked at me with surprise then smiled, asked her daughter something about being outside and going inside and was told they were waiting for confirmation from someone. They looked at me again and instead of them both disappearing, which is what I perfectly expected under the circumstances, they both stayed to talk to me. How was I so fortunate that these two ladies were prepared to take time out of their obviously busy day, to include me and pay attention to me, an unknown floater.

The mother of the bride told me that she was feeling very proud, well of course she was, that was plain to see. I said something about her not just being proud of her daughter on her wedding day but proud of her every day and they both laughed in agreement. Mother said that the day was going well too and agreed that the guests were having fun, again I believed her. There was so much happiness around them all, it was a joy to witness. Mother walked away and I said to my golden friend,

"It is so nice of you to take the time to talk to me, especially as you have guests who need your attention." To be fair there was no one on the pavement who actually looked like they needed anything, attention or otherwise. Perhaps this contributed towards the look of minor wonder on the beautiful bride's face when she replied,

"It's okay, I like talking to you, I like talking to people." Oh bless her. No wonder she was surrounding by so much love.

I tried hard not to take my memory back to the multitude of times in my past when I felt invisible unseen, unheard even by significant people in my daily life. Yet here was I receiving such warm friendly attention from a stranger not just on any day, the likes of which I am happily adding to my encounters on a regular basis but on her wedding day. I mean really, how did I manage that? I do not need to answer my own questions, I just need to know that the whole experience felt good, not just good but very good.

Of course we were not there conversing on the pavement much longer, the beautiful people peacefully disappeared into the pub and then just as if by magic, my bus came moments after the bride left my company. I am blessed, there is no doubt about it.

Phew, that experience made quite an impression on me and now I have no idea how to follow it. Perhaps I should end my book here. Nah, only joking, I have so much more to share.

*

Another time another place another mood, I stood at the bus stop on Garratt Lane when a lady arrived with a less than happy expression, a cigarette in a shaking hand and the other forearm in a plaster cast. She looked troubled and years ago I would have offered concern about her anxiety, allowing her to fill me in with recent events which were probably waiting to be aired and shared. Instead I chose to remember that encouraging anyone to detail the specifics of anything unwanted is detrimental to the speaker and the listener.

The shaking, smoking, wrist splinted lady immediately made a comment on arrival about finding life difficult at the moment, with the use of just one hand instead of two. I looked at her, assuring myself of her well-being, as she looked at me still with her troubled expression. I may have been wrong because of course I could not know exactly what she was thinking. How could I? However, I had the distinct impression that she wanted me to ask about her hand. I did not ask. Not because I did not care, no that was not it at all, in fact I care very much. I care more about her feeling good than she will ever know. I care more about the well-being of everyone I meet and I believe that they are all intrinsically well, whether they believe it, whether they are aware of it or not.

I have not always been of this mind, certainly not. I did not know any better when I began my career in the medical profession. I had no awareness of higher forces during my years and years devoting my blood, sweat and tears to the thousands of patients who held my attention in my nursing capacity. I had no understanding about the negative effects of focus on disease and deterioration, during the days and nights of being surrounded by morbidity and mortality.

Many years ago, I began to make the association between emotional wellness and physical illness. My own health has transformed as a direct result of altering my thought patterns. The physical issues I used to carry around with me are no longer part of my story. Changing my beliefs about my physical body, my anatomy and my physiology, has been instrumental in bringing me to this place of enjoying excellent health. The great thing for me is in knowing that anyone can do this, anyone can turn their expectations around. I discovered the benefits of actively thinking positively, which led me to discover the undeniable link between emotional and physical health. There are considerably fewer people who feel and think like me, than people who live their lives in continued despair, misery and negativity like I used to. I do not even need to fly to the extreme end of the emotional scale to find different thinkers. There are also people who are apparently well off, with homes, family, friends and money yet they are unhappy. I know because I was there, and now they come to me as clients. Often they have no idea what they are looking for, they just know that their lives are not pleasing them.

My lady at the bus stop with the fag and plaster was a long way from hearing any of this but I am glad that I digressed for a moment to say it here. I chose to look at her with a softened expression and simply chose to say,

"You'll be fine." I suspect that she did not want to hear this but it was what I had to offer and it came sincerely from my heart. She turned to another lady and launched into a full and frank account of the events of the previous weekend, involving a random stranger, an unprovoked physical encounter, uniformed personnel, witnesses, statements, what was said, what was done and more. I found interest in the animated way that the circumstances were reported and in how the drama seemed to fill them both with excitement. Some people like this kind of drama, perhaps they do not need to be told that they are attracting more of it by dwelling on the specifics, perhaps they like it that way, perhaps they are happy. The bus came, I smiled at her as I left and she said thank you, wishing me a nice day. I was a little surprised because I had not realised that she was even still aware of my existence. How interesting.

*

The whole drama of life can be easily overheard during conversations on buses. I know that sometimes they are not talking to me but they might as well be, considering the volume and close proximity of voices. People seem oblivious to the presence of strangers, when they openly discuss their business. My experience on bus journeys in and around Richmond, were mostly in relative silence or so it seemed to me. Then I moved to this lively borough and found myself treated to regular discussions about custody, sentencing, appeals, social services intervention, canine misbehaviour, friendship misunderstandings and family turmoil, oh bless them, bless them all. The number 156 can be entertaining when people join after a session at the Magistrates Court in Wimbledon. I have heard people update family members on the phone with details of their cases, speaking loudly enough for the whole bus to hear.

Sometimes the discussions are heart-warming. I overheard a conversation on a number 44 early one Friday morning on my way to Victoria for my beloved morning meditation meeting. A chap was talking to his other half about their little boy, who was upset because daddy had left without saying good bye. The poor man said over and over again that he did not want to wake him which made sense to me, as I was hearing this at quarter past six, so he had a point. Apparently their youngster was distraught so the mother let them speak to each other. This man spent time apologising to his son, explaining that he did not want him to be upset and told him repeatedly that he loves him. Over and over again, I love you, I was close to tears myself, it was sweet and I felt honoured to be in the presence of a man who openly tells his son that he loves him. When he walked past me to leave, I wanted to say something to him but I decided that words could hardly express how I was feeling at the time and feeling good about it was enough anyway.

By way of contrast I remember a couple of conversations which pleasantly reminded me of the colourful tapestry of life. One was on a number 22 from Sloane Square to Putney, I heard a man on his phone talking about his attempts to buy venison, comparing the price per pound in a couple of well-chosen locations. He obviously had a sizeable budget available for food and it was fun listening to his side of the conversation. His discussion included plans for their evening meal with friends and I reminded myself about the importance of expectation and that abundance presents itself in a variety of different ways. In contrast I heard a woman behind me on a number 319 telling a friend on the phone that she had no food at home. She had two pounds to last her until the end of the following week so having no idea how she was going to feed herself until then, she planned to buy a meal that afternoon at a local well known burger in a bun emporium.

*

I suppose the subject of drama is relative, probably akin to the responses of my earlier tales of the bus making contact with four legged pedestrians and street furniture. Anyway, quite different to that I somehow, unwillingly, unintentionally, unexpectedly inspired some drama from a lady who came my way.

I was changing buses in London's unmistakable Elephant and Castle. I guess the locals are used to the experience but I warn anyone of a nervous disposition that changing buses there is not for the faint hearted. Really, I mean it. Never mind, I consider myself fortunate enough to have an adequate degree of confidence, as well as an ability, not to mention willingness, to try unfamiliar things if I feel so inspired.

I loitered in the general vicinity of a bus shelter trying to give the impression that I knew where I was going. I had been given strict instructions by one of my nearest and dearest, someone who cares about me, who advised me that on no account was I to give clues about my lack of local knowledge, therefore not to consider consulting a map or a timetable when I waited. I am not saying whether this advice was necessary, I am not saying that I agreed with it, I am not even saying that I followed it, I simply mention it because it intrigued me then and intrigues me now.

A lady approached a few people near the bus stop, they ignored her or told her to go away and she came to me within a few seconds of me taking up my position on the pavement. The position I chose gave me a clear view of the long wide pavement and the road in anticipation of the approach of my bus. She offered me a leaflet and she said something about it being an opportunity for me to learn more about her religious leader. Well, I was happy and comfortable, she did not bother me and I had no problem with her or her leaflet. However I like to follow my guidance in the moment and my instinct was to say thank you but decline her offer. I was smiling, I was secure, I required nothing from her and was happy to continue my day without incident. What I did not expect was for her to take a step backwards, throw her arms up in horror and start screeching at me. Ouch! What was going on and why was she shouting? A few people at the bus stop turned around. Her exclamation had little effect on me, apart from mild amusement and without me saying anything further she continued, obviously dismayed by my decision to not accept her leaflet. I said nothing, I did nothing, I stayed where I was, unmoved both physically and emotionally. From her place of being clearly incensed she continued, telling me that we are finite and he is infinite as she carried on screaming.

From my place of security I had no desire to justify or defend. From my perspective a stranger offered me some reading material, I politely declined her offer and she exploded. My intention was to stay grounded as she flew off her metaphorical handle.

The screaming, shouting, leaflet lady expressed her discontent, which of course she is entitled to do as after all, this is a free country. Interestingly she did not afford me the same courtesy and vaguely tempts me to question the message that she was intending to give me in the first place. I just looked at her not really caring whether she decided to stay or go. She decided to go. With a glare which seemed to contort her facial muscles she backed away from me, walked sideways to the other side of the bus shelter and continued to scowl at me with piercing eyes. Interesting. I wanted her to be happy but her reaction was not of my choosing. I will never know what inflamed her so much. I have no idea what she actually thought, however, I do know that my intention was from a calm clear place. Perhaps I never need to know why she was so upset by my response.

*

Walking along Tooting Broadway on more than one occasion I have been offered leaflets with the promise of increasing my knowledge about one religious leader or another. Sometimes I accept, sometimes I do not, it is never personal.

One day I was upstairs on a double decker, minding my own business when three guys came up the stairs singing. They were neatly dressed in suits, shirts and ties and as they sounded quite musical I was happy to hear them. Their voices were lovely. They stopped singing, one read a few lines from a religious book, the other two handed out leaflets, one of them called me sister, two stops later, they disappeared about as swiftly as they had arrived. It is never a dull day on a bus and all for less than the price of a hot beverage.

Another day, I was crossing the road in Lambeth one Sunday afternoon, after I had enjoyed a wonderful walk along the South Bank and a visit to the Tate Modern. Close to my bus stop, a small chap, well shorter than me, in a neat grey suit with a grey cable sweater, walked towards me like he knew me. I meet so many people that sometimes I see someone who looks familiar but cannot for the life of me remember from where. He was grinning at me, so at the very least I was expecting a 'hey Carole, how are you, long time … do you remember … how is the …' He stopped in front of me, put his hand on my arm and said,

"Jesus loves you." I laughed and replied,

"Thank you, he loves you too." I am not saying he was surprised but he took a step backwards, reduced the grin to a smile and said,

"Are you born again?" I gave the only reply I had available to me at that moment. Without thinking I found myself blurting out my response,

"We all are darling," and walked away leaving him to think, say or do whatever he wished.

*

I have had many occasions connected with bus travel where people seem convinced that they recognise me. A man walked towards me in front of the 168 bus stop at the beginning of the route in Hampstead. He smiled and spoke first asking,

"Hallo, do I know you?" I did not recognise him yet he said, "You look so familiar."

A man at a bus stop in Wimbledon asked me the same question another day insisting that I looked familiar to him.

A lady at the 176 bus stop in Waterloo glanced in my direction as I approached, saw me and watched me walking, so I smiled and she asked if we had met. My instinct was to say 'not in this lifetime' but decided to keep that option to myself and simply replied that I did not think we had met before. She said,

"Oh you were smiling at me so I thought maybe we knew each other but you were just being nice." How sweet.

*

I wonder if the 'do I know you' question was the inspiration for a couple of mirror incidences which have amused me on different journeys. I was upstairs on a number 19 leaving Sloane Square in Chelsea on my way to Piccadilly, when a lady in the seat in front of me, retrieved her palm sized mirror from her bag and started to look at it while dabbing her cheeks with her finger. So nothing unusual about that you might think. Well ordinarily I would agree. It was her mirror, her face and her finger so it was a common activity to take place. She sat beside the window in her seat and I sat behind her, by the aisle in my seat. My attention was not devoted to her, so I looked around enjoying my journey. When I looked back towards the window, I noticed that her mirror was still raised but not directly in front of her. Oh no, she held it to the side at an angle and in it I had a clear view of the reflection of her face. Interesting. If I had a clear view of her face that meant that she had a clear view of mine. That meant she was looking at me. I looked at her and she stared at me via her mirror and seemed oblivious to the fact that she had been busted. We were making eye contact so with or without a mirror, I did what I always do, I smiled and decided to treat her to the added extra of a little nod. All of a fluster, she looked away and shoved her mirror back into the bag.

Well how funny that the same thing should happen again on another bus a couple of weeks later. The whole person in front, mirror out, angle, view of reflection, smile, embarrassment, fluster, return to bag scenario was another source of amusement to me.

Never mind mirrors, if someone feels the impulse to look at me for whatever reason, there is nothing to stop them. There is no need to go to the embarrassment of demonstrating their lack of knowledge about light and refraction just to get a glimpse of me. For example, let us consider the lady I mentioned on the number 59 from Euston to Brixton when I returned from my fantastic trip to Dublin, she was hilarious.

Then there was the guy in the bright green jacket with matching bright green peaked cap, who sat facing me downstairs at the back of a number 77 one Sunday morning. I was on my way to a lovely restaurant in Ludgate Circus, which (said in my best London accent) does me a right lovely breakfast,

He sat in front of me and made no effort, I mean no effort at all to disguise the fact that he was staring at me. Not just looking but really staring. He kept his eyes on me, looking away for just brief moments before returning his gaze. I did not need to actually stare at him to know that he was looking at me. He sat in front of me, while I looked down the aisle and it required little peripheral vision to know that I was the object of his attention. He said nothing. After a few stops he stood up, he walked to the exit and turned back to look at me. He stepped off the bus walked along the pavement to the rear of the bus and stopped by the window to stare in at me. I briefly thought it might be cool to know what was going on in his mind to explain the silent staring. Then I decided it was probably far better for me not to know.

*

Several times I have sat upstairs with a clear view of the comings and goings
of passengers on the staircase. The first time this happened I was a little
surprised. I became aware of a chap going down the steps, he had stopped
but was not looking down as one might expect and instead his head was up.
I was looking out of the window in the seat directly facing the stairs, so I was
able to notice that he still was not finishing his walk down. I was not sure what
he was doing. He did not seem to be waiting for someone, as no one else
was leaving the top deck at the same time but oddly, his head was still raised.
When you travel frequently on public transport even a few seconds of unusual
activity is noticeable. He was still standing on the steps, no one blocking his
path down, his head still up. Curiosity got the better of me, I made the minor
adjustment of the angle of my head to face forwards and look at him. Oh bless
him, he was looking straight at me. This man had stopped on the stairs to stare
at little me. I smiled at him and bless my soul he looked absolutely delighted.
He beamed back at me, raised a hand with a little wave and bounded down
the steps apparently happy to have been acknowledged. How lovely, all I did
was smile and that seemed to be enough.

So often a smile is enough to set someone off. I love the power of a smile.
A smile can make bad feel good, a smile can make good feel better. How
fantastic is that? Hey, there is no need to take my word for it, we all have
access to daily evidence of the value in giving and receiving this free and
welcome gift.

I was waiting to get off a number 44 at the Summerstown bus stop in Wandsworth. Just as an aside, I have never quite worked out whether Summerstown is actually a real place or if it is just a made up zone to denote the space between Earlsfield and Tooting. Anyway, I was by the door with some people I did not know, they were a trio of pals, two chaps and a lady. As the doors opened the tall blond guy said to his friends,

"Did you see that girl, she gave me a smile." Well for once I knew that he was not talking about me because I had not looked at him. However I was fascinated by his excitement. He continued, "She did, she gave me a smile." One of his friends asked who he was talking about, so he said, "The pretty blonde girl on the bus, she gave me a smile."

I had the pleasure of walking just in front of them along the pavement and continued to hear his joy about the girl who 'gave' him a smile. He would have struggled to sound happier. He said it over and over again and I was happy for him. His friends did not say much but they did not need to because he was enthusiastically sharing the moment.

How could a smile from a stranger have such an effect? Did the girl on the bus have any idea that she had created such a reaction? He was like a little kid all giddy with excitement. If I had heard him carrying on like that a few years ago, I might have wondered about his response to something as simple as a smile. I might have asked myself what the big deal was. Not now though, oh no, now I understand that it can be a joy and a pleasure to give and receive a smile. He had been given a gift and he knew it. I have learned that *'faces which wear a smiling expression are scarce. Some never smile at all'*, Prentice Mulford.

I smile at people a lot of the time and hearing this guy talking about how he felt, made me see it as a good reason to continue. Initially I was not used to it but I wanted to learn. I discovered that it is easy to do but takes practice. I am glad that I took the time to practise because it is paying dividends now.

*

About a year ago I boarded a number 57 at Tooting Broadway one Tuesday morning and sat downstairs at the back. I remember sitting downstairs instead of my preferred upstairs because for one reason and another I had not been out for a few weeks and negotiating staircases on moving vehicles was not a welcome option at that time. I was not feeling one hundred per cent but had decided to make the best of it.

After bleeping my trusty Oyster card, I scanned the area and noticed that seat occupancy was about half but that the middle seat of the five seater at the back was available so I made my way to it. As I sat down, I vaguely noticed a chap hunched over in the corner beside the window, reading a book. I left the seat beside him vacant and sat in the middle as planned. From there I had a clear uninterrupted view down the bus and sat there happy to observe or ignore passenger activity, depending on whatever felt appropriate in the moment.

With my peripheral vision in full working order as ever, I noticed that the hunched book reader had straightened his position, lowered his book and was facing me. He was facing my direction and it was then that I felt him looking at me, it was a strong feeling, strong enough to cause amusement and without turning, I simply smiled, just a little smile, all to myself. It was a smile so small that no one would even notice, or so I thought.

A voice said, "You can stop that right now!" Oh really. The window man had spoken and he sounded so cross. The funny thing was that even though he sounded cross, I had the distinct impression that he was joking. At least it was such an odd thing to say to a stranger on a bus, that I chose to think that he was kidding. I also chose to keep looking ahead and he added sternly, "I said stop it!" I suppose his words may have had nothing to do with me but if I was going to satisfy my curiosity, then I was probably going to have to engage with him. I slowly turned to face him.

Well what I did not expect was to see the face of a delightful man with a bright gorgeous face and the biggest smile, which lit up his handsome face. He was a joy to behold. The words which I had heard did not seem to go with the facial expression which was before me. So I was right, he was only joking and it was certainly an unusual way to attract my attention. If he had said the same words to someone else he may have provoked an entirely different reaction but then again he probably would not have said them.

Anyway, I was looking at him, he was smiling at me and seconds passed before he said,

"Wow, what is your secret?" I had no idea what he was referring to so enquired,

"Secret?"

"Well, there must be a secret for someone to look as beautiful as you." Well, whatever his intention, he certainly had my attention with that statement. It was like watching a Cary Grant movie and I was quite happy to be part of it. I understand how it works and understood that his question was rhetorical. From my point of view the only required response was one of gratitude, so I thanked him. He carried on gazing at me with a dreamy kind of faraway look on his face and said,

"Wow, you look so calm and peaceful, I've never seen anyone looking as calm as you. How are you doing that?" I just smiled. He continued, "I can see that you are at peace with yourself." I thanked him again. It was interesting because when I boarded the bus I had not even noticed him looking in my direction so I was surprised when he said,

"You're clever you know." I waited. "You distracted me from my book. It's a really good book and I was enjoying it but when I saw you get on the bus your beauty stopped me reading." I thanked him again for the compliment. It was lovely to hear him say such nice things about me and sweet of him to not just think pleasant thoughts about me but to go to the trouble of voicing them out loud.

I asked him what he was reading and I enjoyed the fact that his book was about freedom. We had a fabulous conversation, this lovely man shared his thoughts about personal discoveries on his spiritual path and the book was one of many, which he used to increase his knowledge about life and awareness about the link between mind, body and spirit.

I was intrigued, he was speaking my language. He asked me what I do and as I have said before my response varies depending on who is doing the asking. Given our level of conversation thus far, I went with,

"I bring peace." His smile broadened as he replied,

"Of course you do, I can see that you do and I'm sure you're really good at it too."

He did not even ask how, he just accepted my response and complimented me further by saying, that he was convinced that I am good at my work and the people I meet must enjoy the benefit of my skills in helping them. Who was he and where was all this coming from? His comments did not feel like chat up lines, well not to me anyway. Although it has to be said that I am not the best judge and have been told that I am occasionally a little slow on the uptake in that arena. Never mind, all is well, whatever is meant to be will be.

People were moving back and forth but he seemed not the least bit bothered, speaking loud enough for half the bus to hear. When he asked where I was going I told him Wimbledon and he let out a huge laugh saying,

"Don't tell me you're going shopping. I don't think you're just going to wander around the shops, you don't look like the kind of person who does that." I did not really know what he meant by that nor whether it was a compliment. However, he was absolutely right, I am not much of a browser so there was no question of denying it.

The general conversation stopped when he started staring at me again. Something inspired him to return to showering me with compliments and this gorgeous man mentioned my hair, my eyes, my mouth, my face, my posture, my demeanour, my clothes more especially my blouse.

Just for the record I have to agree that my top was gorgeous, lovingly bought for me by my wonderful daughter. It arrived unexpectedly in the post one day and has been a joy to wear ever since. Actually come to think of it, I have frequently received compliments and unexpected attention when wearing this same item of clothing. I wore it to lunch with a friend once and the cute, young, friendly, slim, neatly dressed, Greek waiter complimented my blouse. I found it fascinating because I was lunching with a chap at the time. It was not a date but really, how does attention from a guy even happen when you are socialising with another guy? Actually that was not the first time, as I cast my mind back to a dinner engagement with another male friend when the cute, young, friendly, slim, neatly dressed, half Italian, half Spanish waiter (somehow) asked for my phone number. I found it amusing because I was dining with a chap at the time. Yes, we were friends and it was not a romantic evening but really, how does that even happen? Interesting.

So there I was still on the bus, with my freedom reading, spiritual awakening, peace loving man and his appreciation of little me. Yes, I let him say all of the lovely things which he followed the urge to say. Why would I stop him? All I had to do was listen and it felt great to hear him. I did not make him say any of it.

I spent a lifetime of being a long way from attracting such positive reactions from people, so now that I have totally turned around my experiences as a result of dramatically changing my expectations and beliefs, I am going to enjoy it as much as I can. I do so love to remind myself about the connection between giving compliments and receiving them. I fully understand that not everyone is in the emotional place of feeling able to receive kindness from others in the form of kind words or otherwise but that is okay. It is as it is and people can be as they choose to be.

So by this point the bus was busier, a couple sat beside me, a man sat facing us, a lady sat across the aisle from him, people sat in front of them, there were all of these people within earshot but my new companion talked as if there was no one else around. Interestingly, when he spoke it felt like we were in a bubble and the other people were just moving around and sitting outside, somehow unconnected with our time and space. It was interesting, some may say weird but then so many things can appear to be.

My man said nice thing after nice thing and seemed to work himself into a bit of a crescendo, when he raised his voice in excitement and blurted,

"Oh my god, you are so beautiful, I just want to hold you!" That was the moment I discovered my limit, I decided to make a management decision and stop him. I raised my arm in a 'talk to the hand' kind of fashion and said,

"Thank you very much but that will not be necessary."

He laughed and I laughed and outside our bubble no one seemed to take any notice. We turned the corner towards Wimbledon Broadway and he said,

"I am not going to ask for your number because I know that the Universe will make sure that our paths cross again." I stood up to leave, he wished me a lovely day and our interaction was complete.

What an unusual meeting it was too, even for me that one was pretty special and remains a hard act to follow. I shall leave it up to you to decide what that was all about. My dear children certainly had opinions. Suffice to say, that theirs were quite different from my own. That morning I had left home not quite up to my usual good feeling standard. I had something to do that day, then I did not go out again for another fortnight. I travel this route often and have not seen him since. We met 'by chance' he reflected oodles of positivity then disappeared out of my experience. Coincidence? I think not.

*

Well, not sure how to proceed after that but hey, I have more to share, so I shall follow my impulse to return to the world of compliment giving and receiving.

I stood at my local bus stop for just a few minutes when a lively bubbly young lady flew around the corner at some speed to join me, announcing that she was happy to see me there because it meant that the bus had not gone, which meant that she had not missed it, which meant that she was not late, which meant that she was not as late as she thought she was. She babbled away at me, not even leaving space for a response, which was just as well because as far as I could see she was not making a great deal of sense. There was little point me contradicting her, so I kept my opinion to myself.

She was really quite sweet and without me asking anything, she told me that she was from Spain where the pace was more relaxed, she had lived in England for three months and found that people were continually cross with her for being late. I was not entirely convinced of the possibility of a connection between living there or here and her perception of punctuality but when she said she is really trying to change, a large part of me felt compelled to say,

"No, you don't need to change, you are perfect just as you are." Well even I was surprised when the babbling stopped so suddenly. Not only that, she paused, seemed to be considering some internal dialogue, then as if realising something for the first time, she said in a far less animated manner,

"Yes, you're right, I don't have to change. If they don't like me as I am, then it's too bad." There was a vague possibility that she was referring to a subject not entirely related to time keeping but never mind, the end result was the same. The penny had dropped and that was good enough for both of us.

We enjoyed chatting easily for a short while, well it was easy now that she had calmed down considerably and was not behaving like a marionette with someone else controlling her strings. As sweet as she was, I would have had no desire to contemplate conversing with her in that condition. Soon another lady joined us and I was immediately distracted by our new arrival. We both said hallo to her straight away and she returned our greeting with a lovely smile and hallo too. I was already admiring the beauty of her thoughtful coordination and without giving it much thought, I blurted out,

"Ohh, you look lovely in your purple accessories. You look so well put together, it is obvious that you didn't just roll out of bed." She was smiling and before she had a chance to reply, my Spanish friend chipped in with,

"Yes, I love your purple earrings and your purple eye shadow." Well, I laughed because I had not even notice them. I had been taken by the purple snake skin ballet pumps, purple scarf and purple belt. Okay, now that I am describing it here, the ensemble sounds a little ridiculous but it really was not. She looked magnificent and we were enjoying her outfit. She was okay with our effusive comments and thanked us. I have said it before and I shall say it again, the experience of paying compliments is always more fun when gratefully received but if not, the gift is still sincerely meant. It is theirs to accept in whatever way they wish.

A few more kind words were exchanged then the lovely purple accented lady said,

"You look lovely too with your pretty red scarf and the red trim on your black leather gloves." Well, my coordination efforts were amateurish compared to hers but it was sweet of her and I was grateful for the gesture anyway. Then I brought the Spanish girl's bag into the mix, it was fun and vibrant and suited her exuberant personality. There we were, the three of us, passing round compliments with the greatest of ease, giving and receiving with equal measure. It was a wonderful moment of spreading a little love around.

My bus came first and we parted like acquaintances of lengthy duration, waving hands, blowing kisses and sharing wishes for a joyful day. I laughed to myself that anyone witnessing the scene would never have guessed that we had just met. What fun.

I was obviously on a roll because later that same day I waited at a bus stop in Clapham Junction for my ride home. I spotted a woman wearing a coat of the brightest blue, it was truly exquisite. It would have been difficult not to notice and even harder not to comment, well hard for me anyway. What was the point in me trying to resist the urge? There was no point at all. I had to say something, I was bursting. Of course I did not have to but I decided that it felt better to let it out rather than hold it in.

"Ooh, your coat looks so beautiful, such a gorgeous shade of blue." She smiled a lovely smile which lit up her pretty face to perfectly match the beauty of her coat.

"Oh thank you, I just thought it would be fun to wear something bright on a dull day." Well she was right it was a dull, overcast, drizzly afternoon but I had hardly noticed until she mentioned it. I agreed with her choice of outer garment as the perfect remedy for a grey day, then this lovely lady added,

"Well, you look bright and cheerful too, with your red scarf and your pretty shopping bag." I thanked her for her observation, how sweet of her to notice and to compliment in return. That was not my intention when I fell in love with her coat but we had fun chatting to each other. Her remark reminded me that having been to a local supermarket, I was on my way home with my groceries in my beautiful red bag with the white polka dots. Yes she was right it was a cheerful combo with my scarf. Anyway, never mind our clothing, it was nice to enjoy our lovely easy chat which was also a great way to brighten up a dull day.

*

I am happy to acknowledge that I do not always find the need to comment on the beauty that I see. There has been many a time when I have been quite content to appreciate inwardly, all to myself. I know that thinking nice thoughts has power too and sometimes it feels like enough.

I waited by Tooting Bec Common for a bus home after a fantastic meal in a lovely restaurant. A lady came and sat with me, she wore a beautiful pair of dark green loafers, green plaid pants, a pale green summer coat, a white scarf, (I'm guessing silk) loosely tied around her slim neck. Her hair looked recently styled and her medium sized, bronze, Celtic design earrings perfectly completed her outfit. I smiled to myself to see someone so beautifully turned out. It is no secret to say that when I lived in my previous location, every other person was dressed in this manner. However, no judgement intended, merely my observation, the general mode of dress where I am now is, well, less refined. Either way, I felt no desire to share my joy with her and I just chose to inwardly appreciate.

Seeing this lady reminded me of the time I boarded a single decker in Clapham Junction to make my journey home. I travel this route often and was mildly amused to see two ladies join us. Both with shoulder length, straight, blond hair, wearing tailored trousers, cream blouses, (I'm guessing silk) black, leather loafers with buckle adornments and wait for it … ankle length fur coats. Both of them wore a long fur coat. Yes I have seen long fur coats on a bus in the Junction before but more commonly worn with leggings and trainers on lasses with scraped back hair and hooped earrings. The ensemble before me was more reminiscent of the streets of Knightsbridge.

No amount of telling myself that it was normal to see two ladies so attired in that locale, could really convince me. I loved seeing them and imagined that perhaps they were having a fun day away from their routine on something, which they had heard about, called public transport, you know, just for the experience. I would have been less surprised to see them elegantly exit a chauffeur driven luxury vehicle on Sloane Street.

Well say what you like about first impressions but one of the ladies spoke and my entertainment was joyfully confirmed,

"So this is what it is like inside a bus is it?" Oh how wonderful, I was happy to hear more, her friend joined in,

"Oh yes, it is larger than I expected too."

"Yes indeed, it is rather spacious."

"So how do the people know which way it will go?"

"The driver follows a particular route and the number on the front lets people know where it is going."

"Oh really. That is rather clever isn't it? So how does the driver know when we want to get off?"

"There's a bell."

"Oh really, where is it?"

"We press one of these red buttons and it rings a bell to let the driver know we want to get off and so he knows to stop at the next stop for us."

"Oh how clever."

Bless them both, they sounded quite delightful and I was happy for them trying out the fun of bus travel. I do not expect the experience to change their lives dramatically but I suspect the ride gave them something to talk about for days to come, "do you remember the day when we ..."

*

Eavesdropping on their conversation reminded me of how we take our bus travel for granted. Often the logistics are not clear or obvious to the uninitiated. I met a chatty lady at a bus stop on the Streatham borders who also reminded me of how expectations vary. She spoke to me first by asking if I was waiting for the G1. Well, this is the bus which takes me straight home, practically to my door. I use it often, I know the route well, the drivers are all angels of the road but more, much more about them later.

This lady seemed happy to hear that I was waiting for the same bus and she smiled in response to my smile, saying that she was glad she was waiting in the right place. This was vaguely interesting because G1 was clearly indicated on the sign post and there was a timetable for the route on the information board so she already had proof. Anyway, that was by the by, perhaps she just need human confirmation or perhaps, just perhaps, there as a possibility, that maybe, she just wanted to talk. Ordinarily, there was every reason to assume that her question, my answer and her sigh of relief would be the end of the interaction but I should have known better.

She told me that she was going to 'the hospital'. Like I said, I know the route well and we have the ever popular treat of going into the grounds of not one but two hospitals. I asked her and she confirmed that the one she wanted was indeed on our journey. For some reason after a couple of minutes of looking around and without any prompting from me, she decided to tell me that she had been given the name of the stop for her to get off. Well at this point I was genuinely interested in her proposed plans because the stop she mentioned would have been fine but also required a walk down a residential street, before arriving anywhere on the grounds. It is a large university teaching hospital the site is extensive, it takes time to walk from one department to another so as far as I could see, her most convenient alighting point was dependent upon her destination.

"You can get off at that stop and walk, you look fit, I am sure you will be fine but where exactly do you need to get to? There are six stops within the grounds and it is quite possible that there will be a closer one for you." She produced a map on which someone had helpfully indicated the bus stop on the main road and gone to the trouble of marking out a route for her to a building at the far end of the site. I told her that the map was fine but if she wanted to save herself a long walk there was a bus stop right next to the department which she wanted.

"Really""

"Yes."

"Are you sure?"

"Yes, I travel this route a lot."

"Do you?"

"Yes."

Such a sweet lady and in need of continual confirmation, I did not mind whether she accepted the suggestion or not, she could have walked from anywhere and made it eventually. I just smiled knowing that she would figure it out and make the perfect decision for herself one way or another.

Once again without prompting, within seconds all was revealed. She volunteered to tell me that she had driven from Norwich to London, had parked her car at her daughter's home around the corner and was making the bus journey to the hospital to collect her daughter, who had just had a … and … and … and … All of this information came spilling out, it probably felt like opening a faucet and allowing the liquid to just flow right out. Her drive through the capital was not without its challenges, she seemed to think it was a lot to take on at her age and she was feeling the stress of it. She had forgotten about the congestion charge and was worried about whether she had managed to pay properly or whether she had incurred a fine. Then she let off steam about the roads, the drivers, the traffic, the people, the journey and … and … and …

What she probably needed was a hug but I did not think of it at the time, however what I did do was say,

"You sound as though you did very well. Congratulate yourself for considering the journey in the first place and for managing so well to be here now." She paused as if thinking and found the ability in that moment to agree with me, not just me, she was unconsciously agreeing with what she knew to be the truth but had somehow forgotten.

"Yes you're right, I did do well didn't I? Thank you so much for saying that, I feel much better now." It was my pleasure and it was sweet of her to say that she was glad she had met me.

Our bus came, we boarded, I sat on one side by the window and she sat across the aisle a couple of rows in front. Seconds after departure she turned to me,

"How will I know when to get off, will he announce the stop?" I had already given her the name of the stop more than once but she was clearly distracted with much on her busy mind, so her need for repeated confirmation was understandable. I went into nurturing mode and said slowly but firmly with a gentle wave of my hand,

"Sit back, relax, enjoy the journey and I will tell you when to get off." Oh how funny, she gave another huge sigh of relief, thanked me, sat back, seemed to relax and seemed to enjoy the journey, until I told her when to get off.

As she stood up to leave she asked,

"Do I have to bleep my Oyster card again when I get off?" Well first of all, she must have been more savvy than she had earlier implied, to have an Oyster card in the first place. How did she manage that? Secondly, the question caught me by surprise, I hoped she did not see my look of surprise as another excuse to feel less sure of herself, yet surprised I was. I replied to the negative and as if not content she asked,

"How will they know when I got off?" Once again the question caught me by surprise. I told her that presenting the card to the machine on boarding the bus, pays for the journey, so 'they' do not need to know where she got off. Again she asked me if I was sure, again I answered yes.

Oh bless her, she was a sweet lady who had developed a propensity to find things to worry about. Never mind.

*

I know from my own experiences that travel in unfamiliar cities can introduce us to different ways of doing things. On a bus in New York we made the rookie mistake of attempting to pay for our journey with paper money. We had just arrived, we were tourists, we did not know any better, we were on an adventure. The driver barked,

"No bills only change, no bills only change," then promptly ejected us from the vehicle. That memorable experience was many years ago, made me laugh then, makes me laugh now and I am unlikely to ever forget it. Such fun.

One of my many trips to South America saw us waiting for a bus on the outskirts of a city in Venezuela, when a group of chaps arrived to help us out. They had seen us waiting patiently on the street with no luck and showed that flagging down a bus was a far more proactive experience. One of the guys ran out into the road waving his arms vigorously, almost being knocked down by other vehicles in the process. It was quite impressive and all in the quest to be helpful to English tourists.

Just for fun I am taking this opportunity to indulge myself by recalling a bus trip in the Indian subcontinent. Well if I cannot mention it here then where can I? It was many moons ago, when we survived a glorious adventure of a lengthy bus journey from Delhi in India to Janakpurdham in Nepal. After four hours on a bus full of people, several chickens and at least one goat, I was suffering from the ever increasing need to visit some form of lavatory. I had waited for a long time and we were nowhere near our destination. The driver stopped and signalled to a waist high wall located a few metres away across a field. I made my way, looked the other side of the wall, viewed the hole in the ground and what I saw had the magical effect of eliminating my need to eliminate. My urge was no more. Without another thought I returned to the bus and somehow, managed to last the next four hours, until we reached our goal of a hotel and more acceptable facilities. It is wonderful to have first-hand knowledge of the body's capabilities in performing miraculous feats of self-control.

I have also discovered that bus adventures can be much closer to home, no need to cross the pond although the Americas and Asia will always provide entertainment. Here on our motherland I felt like a proper tourist only up the M6 motorway in sunny Birmingham. Luckily I had coins for the bus and as instructed dropped them into the little fairground style coin collection box, which I was interested to see has a clear panel on the driver's side, for him to see exactly how much has been paid. When the driver is satisfied, the money disappears further below out of view, then the ticket is issued. What I did not expect was that, wait for it … no change is given. Really, no change? I cannot imagine that going down well here in London. To be fair we are only talking about a few pence but what about the principle? I had to quickly, very quickly remind myself that change or no change, it was purely my response that mattered.

Within moments I was back on track and reminded myself that I was in Birmingham for the day to enjoy the adventure. Surprised? So were the three employees at the information desk when I arrived at the coach station. All excited I marched up to them,

"Hi guys, I've just arrived from London to be a tourist for the day. Where shall I go?" Their eyes opened wide, their jaws dropped in unison. One of them managed to muster the temerity to regain his composure and ask,

"In Birmingham, why?" Well, there was little point me trying to explain because I had no real answer other than to say that the previous day I had this urge to book my seat on a coach, then woke up that morning all excited about my day out, leaving my son a note in the kitchen to explain my sudden disappearance.

Not all of my encounters felt the same, I found myself enjoying a delicious breakfast in Café Rouge in the Bullring where the loveliest waitress responded most positively to my decision to visit Birmingham for the day just for funzies. She gave me lots of suggestions of places to go and things to do and even gave the impression of being excited for me. She was a very friendly New Zealander and had been in England for a couple of years, long enough to still appreciate that there is much to enjoy anywhere. Her response was a nice contrast to the chaps I had spoken to moments before.

One of the activities on my list was to play on the local buses so that was how I was introduced to the no change episode. In the afternoon I hopped on another coin eating bus that I liked the look of, going to a place I had never heard of, purely for the pleasure of it. I sat upstairs enjoying the drive past industrial estates, along shop lined roads, through residential areas. I have no idea what I was expecting but the journey was much like being at home and then again, nothing like it at all.

We turned into a road by a row of trees with houses on the other side. Off went the engine so I gathered that we were at the end of the route. My intention was to return to the city but as I had no idea what the plan was for the bus and its driver, it seemed like a sensible idea for me to make myself known to the driver. I did not fancy the idea of being locked on board for an indeterminate amount of time, while he did whatever it was he might do.

Everyone else had disappeared. The driver was still sitting by his steering wheel, so I gave him a cheery greeting adding my tourist status for information. He too was surprised, not just by my (in his words) "odd choice of place to visit" but my travelling by bus for the entertainment, especially to the suburb where we found ourselves at that moment. Well, that was okay because I had little idea where we were anyway. This sweet man from Dudley with his cute accent, gave me some snippets of local info and suggested I visit this and that when I returned to the city. I had already enjoyed a two hour expertly guided walking tour that morning and the driver laughed heartily when I knew things about places in the city, which he did not know himself. During our easy conversation something triggered him to drift into the subject of government, education, closures, deprivation, discipline, parenting, blah, blah, blah. He had a lot to say and I was no longer a willing participant. I backed away and said,

"I have enjoyed talking to you but I am going to go back upstairs now because you sound as though you are going to start being political." Luckily, he roared with laughter, such a nice laugh too and such a handsome face when laughing instead of complaining. He said,

"Oh dear, I've lost you have I?"

"I'm afraid so."

I returned to my upstairs front window seat for the return leg of my trip. When I got off he kindly stopped between stops for me to be as close as possible to the canal for me to try his suggested walk. He held up the bus to chat to me in the doorway for longer than I expected, yet no one seemed to object. He was a real sweetie, it was lovely of him to say that he enjoyed meeting me, it was friendly of him to chat to me for so long and it was my pleasure to meet him too. My other bus journeys in and around Birmingham were fun but not nearly so eventful.

My day trip to Nottingham on the other hand …

*

This was an even more impromptu decision to go on an adventure. I left home early leaving a note for my son again to explain my sudden absence. Arrived at the ticket office early enough to find just a small queue. Purchased my ticket for the first coach to Nottingham and sat back to enjoy the ride. Why was I surprised to see so many people waiting at the gate to board the same coach as me? Why were so many people going to Nottingham of all places? What was the attraction? Perhaps I was missing something. Never mind.

I suspect I was not the only person who assumed the coach would have room to spread out. I walked towards my favourite seat, which looked available when I first scanned, only to find a small person bundled up, lying across the two seats. He pretended to be a pile of clothes but my observation skills detected body parts, so I was not fooled for long. Behind him was another sprawled child occupying two seats and across the aisle were two more pairs of seats taken up by little girls lying across them. Not only was it unexpected to see four children taking up eight seats but they were all roughly the same age, with the two boys dressed the same as each other and the two girls dressed identical. I carried on walking but did not fancy sitting at the rear of the vehicle anyway and there were only aisle seats left as all of the window seats were already taken.

I returned to the apparently sleeping children and could not for the life of me guess who their accompanying adult was supposed to be. By this point there was a queue of people waiting to be seated. Of course I could have sat anywhere, of course I could have let someone else take charge but my instincts were in full flow. I had a seat preference so I decided to go for it.

I looked back and forth only mildly amused by the sea of faces looking up at me as I paused by the minor injustice of the children's positions. It was not then and is not now my place to assume that the other passengers were looking for a spokesperson but my guidance was to take inspired action.

"Okay" I said in a determined voice, "who is with these children?" My enquiry was not rhetorical, it required a response. There was an immediate hush in the vehicle. I looked around, I waited, we all waited. Slowly, very slowly a female figure somewhere in front, rose from a crouched position and turned towards me. I offered a smile, she did not return in kind and that was fine. I was happy to think well of her even if her family of five was currently occupying ten seats on a full coach. I knew all would be well. She looked at me and for a moment I wondered about her appearance of extreme physical and mental fatigue but decided not to dwell on it, as my objective in that moment was to be seated. Without uttering a word her expression implied, "Yeah, what?" Still smiling and from my place of feeling calmly confident I gestured towards her brood and softly pointed out,

"People are waiting for seats." She looked away, spoke in another European language and the children (who apparently were not actually sleeping at all) slowly, very slowly sat upright. Well I am happy to see good in every situation and the upright position helped to free up a few spaces. This was a wonderful response and would have been enough except for the teeny weeny fact that they were still spread out and I still had my eye on the prize, i.e. my favourite seat.

Before I had walked through the door of the vehicle I had already told myself that I did not mind where I sat. I knew how to focus and knew that I could sit anywhere and be absolutely fine. However, I also knew my preference and played with the idea of 'wouldn't it be nice if my favourite seat was free'. It had already seemed unlikely as so many people boarded before me. As 'fate' would have it, the boarding process had been temporarily halted immediately behind me because something technical had to be done with the vehicle equipment. The queue was waiting outside and this is why I had time to walk the length of the coach and back again before there was anyone behind me. From the entrance, imagine my delight when I saw a sea of heads but not in the position of my preferred location. Seeing the boy lying in it was akin to the multitude of occasions when I have driven towards a seemingly vacant parking position in a busy multi-storey car park, only to find a mini lurking at the back of the spot. I know it happens to lots of people and it was hard not to feel more than mild irritation. Anyway, that was back in the days before I discovered how the world works, so that response no longer affects me. I soon learned how to repeatedly find a parking position as if by magic.

So there I was close to bagging my favourite seat and still was not quite there. I could have let the situation be as it was but I decided to continue in my self-appointed role of people organiser. Even though the lady had already turned away perhaps happy with her input, I called in my best cheery I-am-not-irritated tone,

"Hallo there." The coach passengers were all still quiet, no one spoke it was quite comical really. I assume my mother of four knew my call was directed at her because she slowly, very slowly turned from her position somewhere in front, to face me. Once again I gestured towards her little angels and said,

"Perhaps they might like to sit together." With an almost repeat performance she looked away, spoke in another language, a little shuffling took place and my favourite seat was mine, (cue demonic cackle, it was mine all mine). While the beautiful children repositioned themselves, a young lady made an attempt to sit in it but I put my hand on her upper arm, looked into her eyes, smiled and said quietly, softly but firmly,

"I'm sitting there darling." She stepped aside without question, I assume because I spoke to her in my best, you-have-got-to-be-kidding-me-if-you-think-I'm-going-to-let-you-sit-in-my-favourite-seat-after-I've-done-all-the-work-to-make-all-these-places-available. Yes that is it, I am telling myself that is the reason why she did not object. It is amazing how much can be conveyed by intention without the use of words. Anyway, I told her that when the children had finished moving themselves from one place to another, she would have an equally wonderful location for herself and her friend.

Phew, it was quite an eventful start to our journey, all of that going on before we even departed. All I had to do was remind myself that I felt love for every person involved, I set my intention, having no attachment to the outcome, remembering that any response was fine and all would be well.

Just for the record, the long queue of people behind me all chose their places, the coach set off and I was one of only two people on board who had a pair of seats to ourselves. Of course I am not including the driver, of course he did not share a seat, that would just be weird and believe me I rarely use that word.

Interestingly, the Universe sent me an opportunity to increase my ability to focus when I started my journey to Wolverhampton. Again it was another busy coach and I had said my little pre-boarding speech about not minding where I sat but 'wouldn't it be nice if ...' Once again I had been fortunate to bag my favourite position even though the coach was half full when I took my place. A chap sat next to me, young, handsome, impeccably well dressed in crisp white shirt, pressed tailored trousers, polished leather shoes, neat haircut, clean shaven, he looked impressive and I was impressed. He looked at me, I smiled, he spoke. Wow if there was ever a time for me to think that smiling at someone was a mistake then that was it. He asked me if I would change seats, I said no thanks, he then said that his girlfriend was sitting elsewhere and they wanted to sit together. He pointed to where she was. There was one small issue, the seat he was offering was the one position on the entire vehicle that I really did not want to sit in. I said no thanks I was happy where I was, he glared, I smiled, he looked away. Evidently the woman who was sitting next to his girlfriend had expressed her preference by declining their offer to exchange seats too. The love birds were being given the opportunity to demonstrate their adoration for each other from the distance of their seating positions. Words were exchanged between them in another language and I am quite grateful that I did not know the meaning of their discourse. It was an opportunity for me to remind myself that it does not matter what others think about me, only what I think about them. It is okay to have a preference, it is okay to know what we want, it is okay to ask for it and it is okay to accept that everyone can choose. Luckily the event did not affect my dancing in windy Wolverhampton, I had a fabulous weekend and have no doubt I shall share more about it another time.

So back to my journey up the motorway to Nottingham which went quickly and we seemed to be there in no time. I love the journeys, I write and write and write in my notebook and when I am not writing I entertain myself with a spot of cloud busting. If you have not tried it, have a go, it is a lot of fun. My reason for choosing that particular city on a Wednesday was to enjoy a matinee performance of the best musical ever seen, that would be Starlight Express. Just writing those words has the power to fill me with joy. I had planned nothing in advance and simply decided to let the spontaneity of the moment take care of the details for me.

My first task was to find my way into the city centre. A group of three uniformed staff caught my eye, so I strode purposefully towards them to ask for assistance. They greeted me with huge smiles and jolly hallos and it would not have taken much for me to hug them all. I loved their reaction when I told them that I had just arrived from London to visit their theatre on my first trip to their city. At least their reaction was a lot more positive than the Brummie boys. To be fair, I suppose this time I appeared to have a clear objective, although on both occasions my aim was the same, just to have fun.

The two chaps handed me over to the care of the lady as they introduced me to her even telling me her name and saying,

"She is the expert and will be the best person to take care of you." How cool is that? I was talking to absolute strangers in an unfamiliar town and they could not have been lovelier.

They were right, she was a sweetie and took me into the information office to show me maps and give directions for the next section of my adventure. Directing me towards the numbered bay for the bus into the city centre, she gave me lots of wonderful helpful info about timings and locations. She was great but I assumed she had lost her mind and made a huge mistake when she said that the bus was, wait for it … she said that the bus was free. I had to stop her, I needed to clarify,

"Woah, hold on a minute, rewind, rewind. Did you say the bus is free?"

"Yes."

"You mean I don't have to pay?"

"Yes."

"You can't be serious."

"Really, the bus is free."

In retrospect she could have been forgiven for thinking that I had lost my mind because I laughed loudly, doubling over with hilarity.

"I'm from London and that makes no sense."

Eventually, I recovered from my shock and found my bus exactly where she said it would be. Not that I did not believe her because I did but I thought it would be a sensible idea to check with the driver.

"This is my first visit to Nottingham and the lovely, helpful lady in the information office said that the bus into the city is free." When he confirmed that it was, I laughed again, saying that it was a wonderful idea and I told him what I told her,

"I'm from London and that makes no sense." There were several people on the bus and they did not seem to mind my amusement or my conversation preventing the driver from taking off. He momentarily shared my fun, he laughed and said,

"The council provides the service, they pay me to drive the bus, so I drive it." He was an absolute darling, happy and cheerful, not to mention cute.

It took me a long time to get over the shock of the free bus discovery, I was still laughing about it when I chose to lunch in a busy lively Wagamama restaurant. A beautiful waitress understood my surprise because she was from London too and so was already used to the free bus thing. She was about to begin her second year at Nottingham's University and told me about loving her life in the city.

I am sure that I would have been happy anyway but I have a sneaking suspicion that my continued exuberance was in part due to the fact that I had just bought my ticket for the show. I had somehow, as if by a miracle, managed to procure a front row aisle seat in the dress circle. Once again, the Universe was very good to me. I had already decided that I would be satisfied to sit (almost) anywhere. I was taking a chance of course by turning up on spec. I was well aware of that, so if the only available seats were unacceptable to me, I had made the *no attachment to the outcome* decision to let it go and just enjoy my day out, regardless of whether I saw the show or not. To then get the best seat in the house was a massive bonus. I am blessed.

Needless to say the show was superlative. Afterwards I took myself to the tourist office and had a fantastic interaction with a lovely man who seemed happy to share my joy. His beaming smile and bright face welcomed me over as soon as I walked through the door. He looked like a beacon of light and was impossible to miss. I opened with,

"This is my first visit to Nottingham, I've just seen a brilliant show at the theatre, I've got two hours left in your city so what do you suggest?" Well, he was like a man with a project and he bombarded me with suggestion after suggestion, produced maps and leaflets and I was in danger of being saturated with information. It was my own fault really because I had left the field wide open when I asked for suggestions. Bless him, he just went for it. He gave me enough ideas to last for several days, so I narrowed it down by asking where I might find an art gallery to do a spot of browsing. All in all it was a great day out. As far talking to strangers on buses experiences go, the whole free bus episode takes some beating, in the surprising discoveries department anyway.

*

My bus adventures in a wet and windy Wolverhampton offered no such entertainment. One thing I did find sweet was the way the buses replace the destination with one simple word 'Sorry' when they are not carrying passengers. At home they say 'Not in Service' and I remember thinking that 'sorry' sounds so cute.

After a wonderful salsa weekend in a hotel with a confusingly, complicated warren of corridors, I walked just a few paces to the bus stop for the first leg of my journey home. It has just occurred to me that I may devote a future publication to the fun I have talking to various strangers on dance floors, so I shall give that idea some thought for the future. Anyway, a chap stood by the shelter and smiled at me as I approached him, of course I thought nothing of it. He made a big show of stepping out of the way, allowing me room to pass with my beautiful, black, patent, mock croc, designer, wheelie suitcase. Between you and me I adore my suitcase. I have been known to pack it for imaginary trips and travelled to major train stations in full flow of pretending to go somewhere wonderful. Next stop Heathrow airport for my first class flight to my amazing destination.

The bus stop man bowed as I passed and waved me by, somewhat dramatically with a flourish. Okay, perhaps he was simply acknowledging my magnificence and I was happy with that. If he had any other meaning behind his actions, then I did not need to know. I have learned that I can find a thought which feels good in any situation and with that in mind I accept that being treated like royalty sits well with me.

I popped to a nearby shop to buy a drink and snack for my journey before returning to the bus stop. My bowing flourisher was still there and in my absence he had teamed up with a couple of likely lads and I found all of them were sitting on a wall. I was not the least bit bothered by their collection of red faces or their half smoked cigarettes in one hand or cans of lager in the other. They did not much look like they were waiting for transport but more like a social gathering.

My bus came, I boarded, my original flourishing attendant left his mates and joined my bus, telling the driver that he had no money to pay the fare but he stayed anyway. He stood closer to me than he needed to, he smiled and I smiled. He said something, I understood nothing. He said something again, I was none the wiser. It was difficult to make sense of the words behind the slurring. Perhaps I was not trying hard enough or perhaps he had something stuffed between his teeth. Thankfully our journey was short, so I knew that our time in each other's company would be over soon enough. Nothing lasts forever does it, so how difficult could it be to just sit it out and at least be pleasant to my fellow alcohol swilling passenger?

Suddenly he looked out of the window and burst out laughing. Such a nice laugh too his red face and jolly guffaw complemented each other pretty well. When he next spoke, it was as if he were a different person. Suddenly coherent, absent of slur, he said that we had just passed the police station and he had laughed because he saw people waiting outside and he was glad not to be one of them. He seemed pretty happy about that so it seemed appropriate for me to say "well done".

Continuing with his new found vocal clarity, he told me that he likes a drink but he was trying to cut down. I congratulated him again. He assured me that he was not drunk at the moment, even though he was holding a can of alcohol. I told him that it was fine with me either way. I knew in my heart that we all find our own way of reclaiming our power. The greatest gift I had to offer him in that moment was to see him in the fullness of who he is, whether he was aware of it or not. There is power in that. I believe that to be the truth. When I got off the bus he said,

"Thank you for letting me talk to you lovely lady, have a nice day, may the angels take care of you." I thought it was a lovely way to say good bye to a stranger and I was grateful for his thoughtful words.

*

The main reason for my spontaneous day out in Birmingham was partly to see if my interaction with strangers was a London based phenomenon. I am happy to confirm that it appears to be a me thing and not a location thing. I love how often people like to say that Londoners are reserved and other county folk are friendly. I met a delightful lady on one of my many residential weekend meditation courses, who was from 'up north' somewhere and could not understand the unfriendliness she seemed to be experiencing down this end of the country. She was definitely not a fan of London and could not understand my shared experiences of random strangers just finding excuses to talk to me for no apparent reason. She asked me a question, perhaps a significant question, one I did not appreciate the significance of at the time,

"Do you make eye contact with people?"

"Er, yes, of course I do, why wouldn't I?"

That was how I felt then and that is how I feel now I suppose. If this is one of the reasons why people seek out my companionship then so be it.

*

It is time to return to my London experiences. I waited for a bus on Garratt Lane when two little girls ran along the pavement. Their excited playfulness was fun to watch and by the time they arrived at the shelter, they were in a heated debate about who was the winner. The disagreement was clear but it was lovely to observe that neither seemed upset by the other. They just continued to insist that one was wrong and the other was right.

A man caught up with them and they included him in the debate, which was hilarious because he was too far behind to have been a fair adjudicator. Discussion or no discussion they were a happy trio and I had fun listening to them. I looked at the gentleman and as I gestured towards the younger of the two girls I said,

"This young lady seems to be in charge." He laughed and said she is always in charge. I asked if they were sisters and he made me think quite hard when he said that one was the aunt and the other her niece. I have come across that before when children are similar ages and their mothers are mother and daughter. It should be easy to work out but always does my head in, so I decided to leave it alone. I thought it was wonderful for them to have each other for company and he confirmed that they spend a lot of time together. Their friendship was a joy to see.

Another time I was at the same bus stop when a couple arrived with a little boy. The young man read the electronic display and commented on the information with a maturity and confidence, which I have rarely heard from adults, never mind a child. He was impressive. I was impressed. The mother found more than one or two things to fuss about but the father seemed fairly calm. I said,

"That is very good reading." The father smiled and said something along the lines of the boy loving buses and reading signs. Well I had heard him read and pass comments on numbers, timings, destinations and his interest seemed to be about more than a love of buses.

Mother continued to fuss, 'don't do this' and 'don't do that', mostly for no particular reason as far as I could see. The little boy displayed minor irritation with her persistence. I understood. I was intrigued and asked the father how old their boy was. When he told me he was five, I have no idea why but I followed the impulse to say,

"It might be an idea to provide him with a lot of extra reading material because the school may have trouble keeping up with him." The mother said somewhat distractedly, that the class teacher was giving him extra work. This was fine to hear but so not what I meant at all. The father looked at me, he was listening. I have no idea why but followed the impulse to continue,

"The public library has a special section for gifted children. They'll be able to help you find stimulating reading material for him."

Mother scoffed, "Gifted! Oh I don't know about that." The father looked at me, he was listening. Their son was still chatting and reading and mother took time out from her unnecessary repetitions of don't do this and don't do that, to add, "Disobedient maybe." I followed the impulse to offer simply my opinion, that it may appear like disobedience when he has things he prefers and he is prevented from choosing.

"Let him make his own decisions more and the behaviour will improve."

"Do you reckon?"

"I know. Don't give him so much to push against and life will be easier with him." I could see that the father knew what I meant.

The bus came, I boarded leaving them on the pavement, the father waved at me through the window, which I thought was sweet of him. Upon reflection I wonder at my apparent boldness for commenting on their child uninvited and then offering parenting suggestions uninvited but what is there really to wonder about? I followed my guidance to do what felt appropriate at the time. If one quick brief interaction can contribute towards making any moment just a little bit easier for a clever young boy and his attentive parents, then why not. I spoke with love from my heart and whether they heard or took any notice was inconsequential. I had no attachment to the outcome and all was well.

*

I love talking to strangers and I adore the variety of interactions it is possible to have with unknown people. I was sitting upstairs on a big, beautiful, majestic double decker making our way leisurely along the streets of fashionable Fulham. We stopped. I looked down towards the entrance of a mini supermarket. There in the doorway stood a suited gentleman who guarded the threshold. Perhaps this position was his lifelong ambition or perhaps he had dreams of being somewhere entirely different, who knows? All I know is that people walked past him to enter and walked past him to exit and I did not see one person acknowledge him. I tried not to feel sorry for him because really it was none of my business. Yet I did wonder a little at his apparent invisibility. I mused to myself that if I walked past him in the doorway, I would at the very least offer a little smile, perhaps even a salutation.

The precise moment I thought that very thought he looked up. What was he looking for? Had he heard my thoughts? I have no idea but he looked up the side of the bus straight to me and we made eye contact. I smiled. He smiled. When I say he smiled it was more of a grin, which lit up his handsome face. He waved and of course I waved back then as if the choreographed moment was complete, the bus drove off.

I love thinking about that moment, it was special. No words were required yet we communicated just the same.

225

*

I have been fortunate to have other inside-outside bus interactions. I have been waved at, winked at and given the thumbs up by men on buses when I have been on the pavement and from the pavement when I have been on buses. I did laugh to myself however, when I sat at the stop in Clapham Junction one evening when a number 49 pulled up. The next stop for this service is the last on the route and it is normal for everyone to get off here. On this occasion a lady sitting downstairs by the window, saw me outside and smiled. I had no problem with smiling back, I mean why not? The bus emptied except for her, she just stared at me through the pane of glass. I looked away and looked back and there she was with her fixed gaze. It was rather amusing really. Just as the doors started to close she jumped up, frantically pressed the button, the doors reopened and she jumped out. I was sitting down, she walked towards me, stood in front of me, I smiled, she smiled back, then … she walked away.

No I do not know what happened there but it was interesting anyway.

*

I sat at the back of my local single decker and heard the most almighty yawn from the passenger behind me. It was loud, really loud, I could have ignored it but my instinct was to pay attention to it. I turned around to face a lady who looked at me, laughed and apologised for yawning with such volume. I opened with,

"That was quite a yawn."

"Oh I'm sorry it was a bit loud wasn't it?"

"I really felt it."

"Did you really?"

"Yes, I felt the tiredness behind your yawn."

"Oh I know, it's been a long day and a hard day at work." I looked at her as she spoke, I felt her discomfort, I observed her slumped body, I noted her head held low. This poor woman looked so weary.

"Well, it's been really bad at work." Something led me to respond with,

"So leave, do something else." Interestingly she laughed and said,

"Yes, I should, everyone has been saying that." I have to say that I did not know what she meant by 'everyone' but at least the idea had been put to her before. Often people have not considered the possibility of changing jobs.

"So what is stopping you, decide what you want to do and do it." She thought for a moment, then by way of justification continued,

"We've got a new system and we're having problems with it, so everyone is like it."

"It doesn't mean that you have to continue just because everyone else is."

"Thank you, you're right, I'm going to think about it." For the rest of the journey I left her alone. When it was time for me to leave I turned, she smiled a lovely warm friendly smile, I said,

"Have fun with your new system until you leave to enjoy your new career." She thanked me, she actually thanked me, how sweet.

I have many experiences of people finding themselves in careers which no longer nourish and nurture the soul. People feel that their training, knowledge, income, promotions and expectations are reasons to continue when the joy has long disappeared. My own decision to leave nursing after many, many years was met with disbelief and misunderstanding. That was okay, I simply had to believe in myself and understand myself and learn to leave the opinion and approval of others out to the equation.

The new system lady reminded me of a short interaction I had with a guy in a lift. He stepped in just after me and as the doors closed, he let out a somewhat disgruntled moan. This was accompanied by a lengthy yawn, which simply emphasised his hunched upper body and head lowered, demonstrating a discontent countenance. We were in a confined space and my default setting is to uplift and inspire, so it would have been difficult for me not to offer some form of acknowledgement, however small. I had seconds before the doors opened but I know that sometimes a few seconds are enough.

"That was quite a sigh," I said and waited.

Barely raising his heavy head with shoulders still slumped, (if it is possible to be slumped in a standing position) he said,

"Oh I know."

It is not in my nature to probe but I sensed there was more, so I added,

"Long day?"

He said, "You know, sometimes it gets to Monday and I go to work and I ask myself, what's the point?" Ouch! I heard him. This poor man must have felt strongly to say that to a complete stranger. The lift door opened and as I stepped out I said,

"So change it, do something else." Well, I had the immediate pleasure of seeing someone have one of those wonderful light bulb moments. He was still in the lift, he could have gone on his way, he had no responsibility to me but even I was surprised when he used his hand to obstruct the doors and prevent them from closing.

He said, "Do you think so?"

"Yes definitely, it makes a huge difference, I know, I did it."

"Really?"

"Yes sure, it's okay to want to be happy." He was suddenly standing more upright, his head held higher, he looked brighter. The doors tried to close again and he prevented them again. As they reopened he added,

"Do you really think so?"

"Oh yes, if you feel like this you can change, do something that feels better. Do something you enjoy." The third time the doors reopened he just looked at me and I am perfectly convinced that he was thinking something that felt

Carole Chandler

a little better than the thoughts which occupied his mind when he first joined me in the elevator. Whether he stays or leaves jobwise does not really matter, I was just delighted to see him look happier.

*

Bus drivers can have weary moments too, after all they are driving the public in busy towns for a living. It is understandable that they can occasionally look tired. I saw a driver who was slumped over his steering wheel when I boarded. Luckily he moved a little, so I was not overly concerned about his consciousness level. I have seen him before and he recognised me and brightened up, giving me a little raise of the hand as he greeted me. I felt the impulse to say something out of character for me as I usually prefer to highlight the positive,

"You poor thing you look tired, has it been a long day?" Well it was six in the evening but I did start to worry a little when he said that he had just started and was working until one in the morning. I am only kidding I was not worried at all, I knew we were all fine and in safe hands. Sometimes this is how they look but I always feel the inspiration to wish them fun for the remainder of their shift when I leave.

Another driver on my regular route seemed overjoyed to tell me that he was driving the last journey for his working day and pleased about it too. When I said that I expected he was happy that it would be over soon he laughed and replied,

"You're right there, I'm looking forward to going home." What a sweetie.

Then there was the day I saw another regular who caught me a little by surprise with just how tired he looked. His normal smiling cheerful face had been replaced by an unmistakeable expression of exhaustion. I try not to draw attention to it if someone looks less than their best because my experience is that they already know how they feel and attention to the negative simply succeeds in keeping them there or may help them to feel worse. However, as I said he caught me by surprise. I found myself saying,

"Woah, you look so tired, I hope your shift is finishing soon." My poor driver lowered his head and while others boarded, he paused long enough to tell me that he had the end of this run, then a break, then a couple more hours. Well I hoped he would manage to get some well-earned rest during his break because he certainly looked like he needed it.

As fate and fortune would have it, I saw him again the very next day and I was absolutely delighted to see him back to his former normal, smiling, cheerful self. I had to tell him how much better he looked and he seemed happy to hear it.

Another regular driver showed up one Saturday afternoon in charge of my vehicle home and on that sunny day he wore a short sleeved shirt. Nothing noteworthy about that really except that he sported an armful of tattoos. We had previously enjoyed exchanging a few words on other journeys so without giving it much thought I boarded, bleeped, noticed his arm and said,

"Hey, look at you with your illustrated arm, I've never seen them before. I suppose you wore long sleeves but it's summer now." He did not seem to mind my outburst at all and just laughed. We said a few words and when I left we forgot all about his body art, as he told me he was excited about finishing work soon to go home and watch the tennis. That would have been Wimbledon of course.

*

It goes without saying that the personality of a driver can be as different as you or I. There is no expectation for them all to be bubbling over with enthusiasm behind the wheel and by the same token, I do not expect them to all be grumpy either. What I never expected was the entertainment provided by a driver of a number 57 on a cold wintery day from Tooting to Wimbledon. As I stepped towards him, he greeted me with a bright face, a cheerful smile, a happy disposition and,

"Good morning madam," followed by a compliment about my hat. Well I did not blame him, as my hat is rather beautiful. I thanked him and said something about my gorgeous fur hat that I have said many times before,

"I'm nice and cosy under here." He agreed that I looked it and I set off upstairs. On my way to the upper deck, I heard him greeting everyone with a cheerful, not to mention loud, "Good morning sir", or "Good morning madam". I loved what I was hearing. People were responding well to him, saying good morning back, a little laughter here and there and he was cheering people up with his attention to them. A lady boarded with her pram and the driver announced,

"Make way please make way, lady coming through with a pram. Please make room for the lady with a pram." This driver was quite lovely and I was enjoying it.

We set off and our magnificent master of ceremonies announced each stop, not just with the official name but with local information. He mentioned stations, the line they served and destinations, he talked about shops, their old names and new names, he was entertaining and educational and I loved the fact that he felt inspired to do all of this. He was an absolute gem and I congratulated myself for having found myself on his bus in the first place.

We turned the corner for my Wimbledon departure point but I did not want to get off because I was having so much fun. He would not have been out of place on an inner city tour bus, yet here he was taking care of the locals. I had to say something, so I walked to the front of the bus. He greeted the new arrivals just as wonderfully as he had welcomed everyone else and as he looked at me ready to leave, wished me a lovely day but I was not planning to go anywhere just yet.

"I don't want to get off this bus because I have had so much fun listening to you entertaining us all."

"Oh thank you, I'm glad you liked it." Then for some reason I decided to drop into the vernacular. I make no apologies as it is just something I do occasionally when it feels appropriate.

"So are you, like, the jolliest bus driver in the world?"

"Oh I don't know about that but I do try to be happy."

"Well you certainly sound it. If there was an award for the jolly bus driver of the year, you would definitely be the winner." Oh bless him, he seemed momentarily lost for words. I felt I had interrupted his performance for long enough. We shared good wishes and I left feeling honoured to be part of the love he was spreading on our bus that day.

*

I have been fortunate to witness an abundance of nice bus driver occasions which may compete with the performing announcing driver on different levels. He was one of a kind, yet I have seen others performing random acts of kindness.

I sat at the back of a G1, my regular single decker one day on my way home, when in front of me sat a beautiful, slim, neatly dressed lady in colourful clothing. Beside her sat two children calmly enjoying their journey. Not much unusual about that except that the lady carried an acoustic guitar, not in a case and I half expected her to break into song any moment, in true Julie Andrews fashion. Perhaps that was just my imagination working overtime. Never mind, it was not to be. Anyway, there is one section of our journey which has an absurdly long distance between stops, which I suppose is not a problem if you know where you are going.

The bus left a stop on a main road, crossed the zebra crossing, took the second exit of the roundabout, drove a few metres to a side street and prepared to turn right. It was then that the pretty guitar carrying lady looked out of the window, jumped up and called out that she had seen the road she was looking for. Well, I know for sure that the next official disembarkation point was round a corner, along a bit, around another corner, along the road, past the children's playground, through the bollard narrowing section, past the field, turn right, then turn left, past some houses, past the secondary school entrance, then the bus stop. To my mind that is far enough for anyone on a good day, so I expected her to have been a little bit disappointed to have missed the previous stop.

Well imagine my surprise when the driver turned and stopped on the corner, opening the doors for her and the children to get off. She was right where she wanted to be and by the sounds of her gratitude, realised that she could not have been closer. I was impressed not just a little but a lot. This was such a sweet thing for the driver to do. It was my turn to get off a couple of stops later and I was not about to leave without acknowledging what I had just witnessed. I looked at him and smiled first, I always do that so that I have their attention before I speak.

"That was a kind thing you did back there, letting that family off between stops." He tried to dismiss it by saying,

"Oh well, she had children with her." His efforts to minimise his actions were wasted on me, I wanted to give credit where credit was due.

"Yes I know but that was very sweet of you to do something so thoughtful." He smiled, he looked pleased with himself, I hoped he was, I wanted him to be pleased with himself, I was very pleased with him and had satisfied myself that a few words of appreciation from a stranger might be fun for him.

*

Another day, I was on another G1 making my way along the Mitcham Road, when an elderly chap spotted a 355 to Balham and let the driver know that he wanted to catch it. Well, this is the busiest of roads at the best of times and the regularity of buses makes rushing a waste of energy in my opinion. Then again it is only my opinion and I accept that some people enjoy the drama of rushing about or perhaps they have not considered an alternative. Anyway, the driver was so sweet and he diffused the chaps haste by pretending to chase after the 355 in an attempt to catch it up. It set off before he had time to open the doors at the first stop, so he said he would try to catch it at the next one. Even from my perspective of persistent optimism, it seemed unlikely but the old chap seemed happy with the driver's efforts. At the next stop the 355 took off again and I laughed to myself when the driver sweetly said that he would probably make it in time for the next stop. I thought it was hilarious and I thoroughly enjoyed the game.

By the third stop the chap had to get off anyway because our route was to take us in a different direction, to his uncaptured Balham bus. The driver said,

"Sorry you didn't catch your bus mate but I did try for you." The sweet old guy seemed happy with that and thanked him.

When I left I thanked him too for being so sweet to the anxious man and for pretending to chase after the bus on his behalf. He laughed with me agreeing that it calmed him down. It was an act of kindness that few people might have considered but his actions made a difference. I satisfied myself that a few words of appreciation from a stranger might be fun for him.

*

Another day I set off towards a G1 bus stop in an uncharacteristically indecisive mood. My inner dialogue was "shall I walk or go by bus, shall I go by bus or walk?" This is so unlike me and I was still undecided when I stopped to ask a woman at the stop, whether she had been waiting long. I have no idea why I asked the question as I know it is meaningless, as would be any response she might have given me. I asked the question and was obviously was not paying attention because I did not register her answer. With my continued unusual lack of commitment, I left her there and walked on.

Down the road I saw a car in the middle of the carriageway, with the doors open, a girl taking things out of the boot and a woman on a mobile phone frantically waving her free arm. Her phone conversation ended just as I arrived and with her mind on her hand held device, she started pressing buttons as I stood beside her. She looked up at me with an expression which spoke volumes. I asked her if she was okay and she surprised me by telling me that her car had broken down. Well, I know how the world works, cars decide to stop running every day of the week. I understand that, I have been there (she says trying not to think about an unexpected mechanical splutter, then silent engine on Chelsea Embankment at one o'clock in the morning). My point is that there is never a convenient time or place for a vehicle to render itself inactive because your whole reason for being in it, is with the intention of going somewhere else. What surprised me was her position in the road. So I said,

"You broke down there?"

"Oh no, we broke down around the corner, I pushed it round here." Apparently something had seized up and she was unable to push any further, so there it was in the middle of the road. I congratulated her for managing to move it as far as she did because I am not sure that I could have done. I am not entirely sure why but saying these few words seemed to help. Looking a little less flustered, she sighed (again) and thanked me. Then she continued,

"I start a new job today and I'm supposed to be dropping my daughter off and I've got these parcels to deliver first and … oh what a way to start the day!"

Well I could see that this particular Monday was succeeding in trying her patience. She had a bilateral arm waving thing going on and I knew that there was no point me joining in with her despair.

I had no idea what I was planning to do or say to be honest. I did not have a plan at all, mostly because of her agitated state. I had no idea whether she was in any condition to offer me her attention for more than a moment, for me to attempt to induce calm within her. A moment of calm was all we were looking for, well it was all I was looking for on her behalf. I know from my knowledge and experience that if she could somehow find a moment to quiet her mind, even in the midst of her perceived dilemma, it could be powerful enough to make her frantic phone calls more efficient and also allow good things to happen.

I maintained my emotional balance, looked at her, paused and said,

"Just stop a moment. It's hard for you to think clearly or make decisions when you feel like this." She did stop. That was a result. She looked into my eyes as she lowered her arms. Well perhaps she was not as far gone down the road of the Monday blues as it appeared. Perhaps I could risk it and try something else. She was still, she was looking at me, she was quiet, she was waiting, I started to speak,

"Take a ..."

Her phone rang. She will never know what I was going to say. She looked at her screen, put her hand on my arm and said,

"I have to take this, thank you for your help," then attended to her call. Ooh, we were so close but then again, probably it was enough.

Cars had come and gone, seeing her in the way they reversed and rerouted or drove on the pavement to drive by. At that moment a bus came and stopped behind her. Obviously it stopped because she was blocking the road. When I assessed this new situation, I realised that I had an opportunity to return to the bus stop with plenty of time to spare because the stationary vehicle in the middle of the road was creating a situation in my favour.

Moments later I found myself back at the bust stop, in the company of the lady I had spoken to earlier. She was blissfully unaware of the goings on until I returned. While we were talking, I looked back to see the bus driver was pushing the lady's car down the road to a more convenient place for her to await assistance. Oh bless him for helping her, he was kindness itself and had made his thoughtful decision within seconds of seeing this damsel in distress. How wonderful to know that people like him exist. How wonderful to know that someone like him would be driving me.

I was soon to discover once again that some people view situations slightly differently to me. I said how sweet I thought he was to help but my bus stop companion was quick to tell me how drivers are unhelpful and do not care and are unfriendly and ... and ... and ... Well I was not having that, so I went into defensive mode, saying that I have had many experiences quite the opposite of what she said. That was then and this is now and frankly I would not bother to contradict similar comments if I was to hear them again. Bus drivers do not need me to defend them. In fact nobody needs me to defend them. I knew it then but I must have forgotten that the woman spoke merely of her personal experiences, of life from her perspective. Her comments were all valid and a reflection of her expectations. My life used to be like that too, it is quite different now.

The bus arrived, she boarded without saying a word but there was no way I could be persuaded to ignore him. I simply had to say something about the scene I had just witnessed.

"I saw you pushing that lady's car, it was very kind of you to help her."

"Oh, it was nothing." His efforts to minimise his actions were wasted on me, I wanted to give credit where credit was due.

"You really helped her, she was quite upset when I spoke to her but I am sure that what you did helped her to feel better."

"Well, it was easy really."

"Perhaps, but you stopped to help. You are an angel for doing that and I know she is really grateful to you for being so kind."

He smiled, he looked pleased with himself, I hoped he was, I wanted him to be pleased with himself, I was very pleased with him and had satisfied myself that a few words of appreciation from a stranger might be fun for him.

*

Another day, another bus, this time on a 333, we were making our way towards Amen Corner on the borders of Tooting and Streatham. The bus had stopped, the embarkation disembarkation procedure was complete and to all intents and purposes we were set to leave. I had the good fortune to be sitting upstairs at the front and from my excellent vantage point I had first-hand knowledge of why we were not moving. About fifty metres away, a man was frantically waving and running towards us. Now before I incriminate myself, I will be the first to admit that my fifty metre estimate may be off by a small or even large proportion. However, the exact distance is not critical but it is safe to say that he was a fair distance away moving at quite a pace and gesticulating. As if that were not sufficient, he had the hand of a little girl in tow. She ran really well to keep up with him or he ran well to keep up with her, I am not sure which, either way, they both ran and the bus waited.

Anyone who travels on London buses knows that there is an entire testimonial right there all by itself. So much so I feel the impulse to repeat it, the bus waited. The driver stayed right where we were, until the man and the little one arrived puffing and panting and excitedly grateful. It was a joy to witness, I was glad to be there to see it. Yes I have seen kind drivers wait on many occasions and it is always a delight for me. I have lost count of the many times I have been on the receiving end of this thoughtfulness, drivers frequently wait for me and I remember never to take it for granted but I am fully aware that the story is not the same for everyone. Each person who enjoys or endures (depending on their perspective) this mode of transport in this part of the world has a story to tell about a passenger being at the door of the vehicle at a designated collection point and the driver mysteriously for whatever reason, takes it upon himself to release the brakes and leave. Not this driver.

When it was time for me to depart I simply had to say something. Of course I could have made my exit through the middle doors and gone about my merry way, without giving the incident another thought. Of course I could have taken the easy option but I love talking to strangers and I love acknowledging goodness, however slight it seems. I stood at the front, made eye contact and smiled so that I had his attention.

"That was kind of you to wait for the man and his little girl when they ran for the bus back there."

"It was nothing." His efforts to minimise his actions were wasted on me, I wanted to give credit where credit was due.

"Well, it was thoughtful of you and you did not have to do it but it was nice that you did."

He smiled to himself, "They looked like they were in a hurry."

"It was a really helpful thing to do and very sweet of you."

He smiled and looked pleased with himself, I hoped he was, I wanted him to be pleased with himself, I was very pleased with him and had satisfied myself that a few words of appreciation from a stranger might be fun for him.

*

Just to set the records straight I would like to speak up for drivers using their initiative to make wise decisions and also know when not stop. Another day, another bus this time a number 44, I was on my way home after a fun tango lesson in central London. It was late, it was dark, it was cold and I really wanted to go home and curl up in my warm bed. I stood up to leave at my nearest stop on Garratt Lane, when out of the window, around the immediate vicinity of the bus shelter, I saw and heard a group of young adults of mixed gender, creating an almighty hullaballo. The bus started to slow down and I am perfectly convinced that I was not the only person on board who was wondering what the hell was occurring outside.

We were about to stop. I was about to get off. I was on the verge of walking into 'that', whatever 'that' was. I reminded myself that I could choose what to think. I reminded myself that I expect things to work out well for me. I stood at the top of the steps, closed my eyes, took in a deep breath, relaxed into the sensation of the bus slowing down, then… felt the bus pick up speed. I opened my eyes, we were still on the move, we were accelerating and we flew past the mayhem makers without stopping. I sensed that on board, we were united in our relief. However, it was not over. We may not have stopped but we were not invisible. The members of the pavement posse were unimpressed and signalled their dissatisfaction by screaming at the driver, running after us and hurling an assortment of beverage containers at our windows. It may be safe to assume that the glass vessels were for alcoholic liquid refreshment.

For the first time ever in my experience, the bus did not stop and no passengers complained. By the next stop, the chasing party had long given up, so we were safe to depart. Several people left but I was once again so grateful to the driver, that I felt no need to keep it to myself.

"Good call back there."

He smiled, he knew what I meant, he smiled and said, "It was a snap decision."

I continued, "I think it was a great decision, well done, I appreciate your quick thinking."

He smiled, he looked pleased with himself ... if you have been paying attention you know the rest.

*

There have been times when I have had a little harmless fun with bus drivers and it is always well received. Like the time I rode a number 77 from home to Waterloo, early one Sunday morning. From my upstairs front window position, my attention was soon captured by the driver's motoring style. He took off early before traffic lights turned green, he kept going when they had already turned amber, he ignored more than one that was already on red and seemed to be playing more or less his own little game. Needless to say it was the quickest journey I have ever known and thankfully I felt good about myself and the world around me, so found the experience amusing. At the end of the route I would ordinarily have thanked the driver before leaving anyway but I felt like having a little fun this time.

"Thanks driver." I paused before continuing, "So … you have an interesting relationship with traffic lights, don't you?" It was not really a question, I was making a statement.

Without looking at me he replied, "The roads were quiet and I know the junctions well."

"That's fair enough I suppose, at least you got us here safely." I was glad to hear his response,

"You were all safe, I don't take chances, I knew what I was doing." Enough said.

Then there was the time I had some unexpected fun with a driver on my way home one evening. Just as I was preparing to leave I looked for my trusty Oyster card to have it ready for my next bus and totally out of character, I could not find it. I am not a 'where's my key?' or 'where's my phone?' or 'where's my card?' kind of person, I am organised, focused in the moment and take my time, without clouding my mind by rushing around, so I generally know where my things are. Unusually for me, my card was not where I expected it to be. I searched my bag and pockets then stood up to look around the seat and on the floor. I was not unduly concerned because I expected it to appear any moment, so when the bus played its 'this bus terminates here, please take all your possessions with you' announcement, I knew that we were at the last stop. Just as instructed, I was trying to make sure I had all my things with me. My search continued. I was upstairs alone when the lights went out and the bus moved off. Understandably, the sudden darkness did little to assist my efforts. Just for information, I frequently keep my Oyster card well topped up, usually with upwards of thirty pounds, adding fifty pounds on occasions and I once had around seventy pounds on it, just to play with the feeling of abundance, which was fun for me. Well, with this in mind I was going nowhere without it. I continued to grovel around in darkness hoping that my hands were not going to make contact with anything too unsavoury. The Universe must have been playing with me because I found my card in my bag in the internal zip pocket, precisely where I usually keep it, where I had looked (and looked and looked) before. With my search over, I was ready to leave.

I expected us to be heading for the usual place where this bus stops between routes but when I looked out of the window, I was surprised to see that we were heading in an entirely different direction. We were moving at a brisk pace and I had no idea where he was going, so it seemed like a sensible idea to make my presence known to the driver. Well I do not plan to repeat this event but if I ever find myself in that situation again, I will ensure that I make some noise before I unexpectedly stand beside him and say,

"Hallo driver, I was upstairs looking for my Oyster card and I didn't want to leave without it." I am not sure how much he heard because he jumped and coughed and spluttered and I think we are both lucky that he did not have some kind of coronary incident, as a result of my sudden appearance. It turned out his coughing and spluttering was due to the cheeky fag that he was enjoying in his presumed solitude. He hastily extinguished it when I sprang upon him from nowhere. No of course I did not mind, it was no business of mine and yes it could be our secret. I expected to jump off the vehicle as soon as we reached a convenient spot, then the darling asked me which way I had intended to go. With all of the commotion, I had not even realised that I was on my way home, so bless his heart, he took me as far as he could and made an unscheduled stop for me, before turning round the corner. Well how about that then, I had a free ride home, met a lovely friendly chap and enjoyed another personal driver experience on an empty bus once again.

There is something particularly special about having a personal driver. I am reminded of the day of another media inspired mass hysteria event in London, which attracted hundreds and hundreds and hundreds of flag waving jolly people all walking in the same direction. Not for the first time I was alone walking the opposite way, I had something to do which was not dependent upon constitutional celebrations. There were hardly any vehicles about but buses were running and I was walking along Charing Cross Road past Cambridge Circus heading north, when something prompted me to turn around. There coming towards me was a number 24 to Hampstead Heath, which was my destination. I was not at a bus stop and I have lived and travelled in this town long enough to know, that hailing a bus between stops is not the done thing, not to mention probably a waste of time because, well, they just do not stop. Despite knowing all this, I felt the urge to put out my hand. Perhaps I was feeling cheeky or just lucky. The driver pulled over, stopped, opened the door and I jumped on. To this day I remember it as one of the most remarkable things that has ever happened to me. Of course I thanked him and thanked him. I wanted to acknowledge how kind it was of him to bend the rules for little me. I sat upstairs at the front. I had the whole bus to myself, for the entire journey.

I enjoyed the pleasure of a personal double decker bus and expert driver all for me. I felt extremely regal sitting in my glorified throne position and I could not help thinking that a few miles away, the crowds were gathered to watch a cavalcade but from where I was sitting, I was an integral part of a royal procession that I could get really excited about. At the end of the route I had a little fun with the driver,

"Wow, I had the bus all to myself, how lovely is that?"

"Yes, I was your personal driver."

"Thank you I'm very glad that you were too." Such a wonderful man, it was a pleasure to meet him. I may be wrong but I get the impression that he enjoyed the distraction.

*

Then there was the time I found myself at an unfamiliar location somewhere between Oval and Stockwell, after breezing through Elephant and Castle or the Elephant as it is more affectionately known. For one reason or another I found myself drifting between an 88, 155 and 333 because I had initially set off for home but then decided to pop to my favourite café. So there I was, when a double decker slowly pulled up beside me, I did not move as he gently, slowly, inched his way forward until the door was right in front of me. It was not too far ahead and not too far behind, just right. The doors opened and I was greeted by a handsome driver with a gorgeous smile and I am reluctant to say yet again that his bright smile lit up his face. Hey, what can I tell you except that it did, it really did. I smiled at him, raised both of my arms, pointed my index fingers ahead of me at waist level and said two words,

"Just perfect." I was referring to the accuracy of his stopping in the perfect position for me to board and I knew that he understood as he laughed a cheeky little laugh and said,

"I do try." However, if he had thought I meant that his lovely smile and handsome face were just perfect then that would have been okay by me too. Anyway, I said,

"Thank you for trying, I appreciate it." Once again, a bus driver looked pretty pleased with himself and although it seems a brief insignificant interaction, I am simply having fun including it among my many joyous experiences.

Carole Chandler

Years ago back in the days when I was less sure of myself, I would have been unlikely to enter into unsolicited dialogue with unknown people, for fear of my intentions being misunderstood. How funny now that I have no concerns in that arena, as a consequence I encounter no misunderstandings either.

Well not usually...

*

It was a bright sunny day and I jumped on a double decker on my way to my favourite art shop on the Mitcham Road. The handsome driver was wearing a pair of smart sunglasses and in his crisp white shirt sitting by the steering wheel, he did look fairly grand. I said hallo and without pausing I simply added, "Cool shades" and went straight up the stairs forgetting all about it.

Approaching Tooting I remembered that I had been caught out before when on a less familiar route because with so many buses passing through, some of the stops are staggered. I knew where I wanted to get off and did not fancy going beyond it because I would have had to walk back along the busy high street. Sometimes weaving my way in and out of the crowds can be fun, sometimes it is not, I prefer to be in the right frame of mind or not bother. It made sense to check with the driver, of course he would know, so that seemed the most sensible course of action.

With no ulterior motive I went downstairs and stood by the driver ready to ask my question. He looked pleased to see me but that was fine because I am used to people being pleased to see me.

Woah, hold on a minute. I have just experienced a twinge in my emotions for a moment there as I wrote that. It seems not so long ago when the opposite was my experience. I am so glad to be writing this stuff down. I want people to be open to the possibility of changing the way others respond to them. If your relationships are pleasing you in every way then congratulations

255

and change nothing. If however you find yourself wanting your experiences with other people to be different, then my intention is to offer a glimpse of possibilities. It is possible to effect a major change.

Where was I? Ah yes, the driver said hallo and I asked him whether he stopped at the stop I wanted. He said yes which was great and I started to walk away. He called me,

"No stay here, you can wait here." How sweet of him, particularly as I was conscious of talking to him while he was driving, I did not want to be a nuisance. He was already smiling then said,

"So you like my glasses then?"

I thought nothing of it and replied, "Yes, they look good."

With a coy tilt of the head he added, "They look good on me do they?"

Okay, between you and me I have been accused by friends and family of being a tad naïve when it comes to boy meets girl opening banter. Actually come to think of it my naïvity seems to extend to girl meets girl opening banter too but perhaps those are stories for another day.

The driver's words were simple but even for me there was no mistaking the tone of his voice and the manner which he had mysteriously adopted. You know the one. Well, I was not interested. I had to nip it in the bud. I looked at him without a hint of shyness, no bashfulness from me, I said boldly,

"Yes they look good on you, I think you know that already and you don't need me to tell you." Oh bless him for feeling the impulse to continue with his trend,

"Hey, perhaps you'd like to buy me another pair." Well he was being quite ridiculous and I could only assume that he had lost his mind.

I told him, "You don't need me to buy you anything, I can see that you are quite capable of taking care of yourself." It was clearly time for me to leave so with a smile and a thank you, I left.

*

In case anyone is wondering, let me just clarify that I am open to possibilities. I like to remember that I have no idea what is in store for me, so I continue to have my preferences and like to go with the flow.

I boarded a bus one Saturday morning to go to work and thought I had hit the jackpot when I saw the driver. Ooh he was cute and I suspect I took a little longer to bleep my card than was absolutely necessary and would have adored the opportunity to gaze into his eyes for as long as time exists. Alright perhaps not that long. Did I say anything over and above my usual greeting? Not out loud anyway. It would not have been ladylike to say what I was thinking. Did I at least change the tone of my voice and elongate the vowels in a Marlene Dietrich kind of way? No, not that either. What I did do, was sit where I knew he could see me in his mirror, instead of where I usually would choose to sit. What was I thinking? He probably had not even noticed me. Even if he had, he probably had no intention of checking me out in his rear view mirror. Give me a break, a girl can dream can't she?

When time to get off, I ignored the exit door and walked to the front, just for the pleasure of one more glimpse. I said thank you, made eye contact and smiled. None of that was unusual for me, except for the moment when I tried not to swoon, however the pleasure of looking again at his handsome face was an added bonus. What did he do? He winked. He winked at me. That wink made my day. The effects of that wink lasted all day and the next and the next. It was about a week until I stopped thinking about that wink and now that I am retelling the journey, I am living the joy of that wink all over again. Memories are wonderful. The trick is to know which ones are beneficial to remember.

It is often fun to observe how experiences, circumstances and events occur. There is a driver who is a regular on one of my local routes and it appears that I have had the pleasure of seeing him a disproportionate number of times. Three times in two days a couple of weeks in a row, feels like a lot to me. I was just walking along the road one lunchtime, when he passed and we waved, then hours later a few miles away, I was surprised to see him again. It was a pleasant surprise and fun to share another greeting. About a week later I mentioned to a friend over lunch, that I was amused by the fact that I had seen the same driver so often. I mean really, what are the odds? We had a bit of a laugh over it, then on my way home my bus arrived and to my amazement there he was at the wheel again. As if that was not enough, I saw him the next morning, when I was out for one of my meditative morning walks. He was a real sweetie and stopped the vehicle to hang out of the window to pass pleasantries with me on the other side of the road. Bless him for being so friendly. I always appreciate kind thoughtful attention.

He is not the only one who has drifted frequently into my experience. How lovely to get on a bus one day and see the face of driver I had not seen before. Not just any face either, he looked like a cross between Patrick Kleivert and Jeremy Guscott, not that I have seen either of them for about fifteen years. I am trading upon memory but this guy reminded me of how they looked then. No reason to assume that they have reduced their level of cuteness over the years I suppose. Anyway, this was my immediate impression along with something not too far away from, "woah, what are you doing driving buses, shouldn't you be at a photo shoot somewhere?" Safe to say I kept my thoughts to myself and maintained my familiar composure with a simple hallo.

Some weeks later I mentioned him to my daughter, who failed to be the slightest bit impressed, as she knew neither Patrick nor Jeremy. Never mind, I have enjoyed the pleasure of seeing this driver several times too. One day he drove my bus in the morning as well as that afternoon and I had the unexpected delight of bumping into him while out shopping. Ooh lucky me.

*

My local drivers are angels of the road and I can share many experiences of their kindness and thoughtfulness during my journeys to and from home. Just to offer a few examples, I have enjoyed lovely greetings, waves and toots when walking. I have been picked up between stops many times. I have been dropped off in an undesignated area right outside my front door a number of times and that is always, absolutely always, an extra special treat. Once I was walking along, nowhere near a pick up point and one driver kindly pulled up beside me to ask where I was going and whether I needed the bus. Well I was so touched then and still am when I think about it. That was unbelievably thoughtful and contributes to my lasting impression that people generally mean well and the world is a good place.

I sometimes have to remind myself that I live in a busy part of London, even though it sometimes feels like I am enjoying the sensation of village transport. I could easily be mistaken because some of the unusual personal events which pass my way, I would have previously associated with faraway places. Like the time we had fun on our family holiday touring Cornwall by bus, yes that is right, without a car. I remember the joy of being on a bus on our way to Falmouth, when a lady told the driver that she had missed her stop. From my knowledge at the time I would have been pretty impressed if he had simply stopped to let her get off but he took a detour and drove back round to retrace some of the route, so that she could be where she wanted to be. What kind of Samaritan was he? The locals on the bus told us what was going on because we had no idea that he was going out of his way to be helpful. We had all the time in the world, we did not mind, the other passengers did not complain either and all in all it was a learning experience for me. I did not think that kind of thing could ever happen in London but I guess I have discovered otherwise.

Of course it is not all rosy and my locals feel comfortable enough with me to share one or two challenges. One of the drivers told me that he counted the number of humps and bumps on his route (ouch, 93!) and planned to share his findings with his manager. He had my sympathy. Another driver told me that he has nowhere to buy anything to eat or drink where he has his break. He had my sympathy. Another driver told me about the time he was reprimanded by the controller for taking longer than scheduled on his shift, when he drove on a day of snow covered streets. He had my sympathy. Come on managers, how about taking care of our drivers. Surely if they are happier in their work then everybody wins. I am not the only person responsible for keeping them jolly, am I a single handed campaigner? I think not.

*

I boarded a local bus one weekday morning at 6.35 on my way to Wandsworth Common for another of my morning meditative walks. The driver saw me first and was obviously feeling playful because when the doors opened, I stepped up and saw him with both hands, fingers laced in front of his face. What was going on? He moved his hands and revealed a big cheesy grin on his bright handsome face.

"Hey, lovely to see you, are you on holiday?" Well, I had a very good reason for asking what may appear to be an odd question. The fact is that he used to be a regular on the route until transferring to an alternative about a year ago. How did I know he had transferred? Easy, he told me. How did he tell me? Did he tell me in advance? No. Was he a friend of mine? No. Did we have mutual acquaintances? No. How then?

Several months ago I had just passed the traffic lights on the junction of Gap Road, Plough Road, when from the queue of vehicles I heard the toot of a horn. I chose not to acknowledge the sound and continued walking. The repeated hooting tooting did not persuade me to take more notice either. It was not until it was followed up by a loud "Hallo", that it occurred to me that somebody, somewhere was being quite persistent and that there was a vague possibility that perhaps, just maybe I was the intended object of someone's attention. I turned towards the line of cars waiting at the red traffic light and leaning out of the window of a car, was a handsome young man waving enthusiastically at me. I must have looked unsure because he yelled,

"Bus driver!" It was then that I recognised him and waved back thinking that it was so sweet of him to go to so much effort to attract my attention. He could have just as easily seen me walking, recognised me, said so to himself, then turned his attention to something else entirely. However he went to the trouble of wanting to be seen and engage with me. I was flattered. I was honoured that someone of such brief acquaintance considered little me to be worthy enough of such interest. I called back,

"Oh hallo there, I recognise you. You're out of context!" He laughed a hearty laugh, shouted back that he had changed routes so was working in a different area. Oh how friendly of him to give me information. The traffic lights changed and he made the sensible decision to proceed and not hold up the traffic behind him any longer.

Returning to my aforementioned early morning bus ride, all that was to explain why I asked him if he was on holiday. I knew it was not his regular route anymore, so I thought it might be fun to refer to a Busman's Holiday in its literal sense. We enjoyed a lovely chat, he was working overtime and I just thought it was fun to think about how our paths had crossed once more, giving us a chance to interact again. I did not intend to stand at the front and talk while he drove but he called me back when I made a move to sit down.

As luck would have it I saw this same driver again a few weeks later. What are the chances? Of all the drivers, in all the buses, in all the towns … I thought to myself in true Bogart style. I realised recently that I have never seen the movie Casablanca but it appears to be responsible for a plethora of familiar quotations. We enjoyed another friendly comparatively lengthy chat. He was gracing us with his presence on this route, this time to accommodate a shift change, cheerfully telling me about his new car. All in all, it was easy to see why he looks so handsome, gorgeous and lively whenever I have the good fortune to see him. I concluded that his naturally cheerful disposition is a contributory factor.

*

I learned something else about expectations when enjoying a chat with others who we do not know well. There is a driver who I have had the pleasure of seeing on several occasions, he is invariably friendly and willingly chats to me. One day, he paused the bus on a corner by a shop where he obviously knew people. They called to him, he called to them and I laughed to myself when I heard him speak. He dropped into the vernacular and used vocabulary and intonation which he had not employed with me. I hardly believed it was the same person speaking.

Further along our same journey he stopped beside another bus, travelling in the opposite direction, he talked to the female driver, she spoke to him and once again his words and tone were in complete contrast to how he had chosen to verbally express himself when communicating with me. How interesting.

*

Then there was the lovely lady driver who I saw a couple of times who delighted me with her friendly manner too, such a pretty face and a gorgeous smile, she looked happy in her work. I hopped on a bus one day and after sharing a greeting I noticed that her hair looked different so it seemed only natural to mention it. Well, I would be inclined to comment if I noticed that a man's hair had changed but it is even more fun to acknowledge other women because we love it when our hair is noticed, don't we girls?

This occasion was no exception and I was so glad that I did mention it because while laughing, she told me that she had celebrated a birthday a few days previously and her hair had been transformed with extensions as a treat. I was happy to see her beaming a big joyful smile as she told me about it. It was a fun to chat and laugh with her.

*

Most bus drivers are men, I suppose that makes sense from my, I've-never-driven-anything-bigger-than-a-small-van perspective. However, there are female drivers, of course there are. Perhaps I have no reason to expect them to drive differently but I do and my experience is that they drive the same as the guys. Then again this is my experience and I am well aware that my experiences differ from the majority, hence my inspiration for these writings. One afternoon, I congratulated a lady driver for handling a bus expertly around a tight corner with another vehicle awkwardly parked in our way. She dismissed it as nothing and I questioned my motives for offering the compliment in the first place. Then I remembered that regardless of her apparent response I had nothing to worry about. I did not comment because she was a Sheila at the wheel, I would have been just as inclined to be impressed if there was a Bruce in charge of the controls. Well I like to think so anyway.

What about the time when a driver waited behind a van, which had obviously been momentarily abandoned by an absent minded driver in the grounds of our local hospital. Our driver waited but no one came which was a surprise for all of us because it was blocking a one way road. He decided to proceed cautiously. I thought I had a pretty good view and as far as I could see there was little chance of him making it through unscathed. I could not look. I did not dare allow myself. It was tight, it was really tight. It was close, really close. I had convinced myself he was not going to make it. I was in no hurry to hear the inevitable sound that was sure to confirm my suspicions. I maintained my attention on the other side of the bus and out of the window I found something, anything to focus on, other than what was keeping all the other passengers entertained. I still do not have any idea how he did it, other than to assume that he was some kind of magician. When I left a few stops later I congratulated him.

"Well done for squeezing past that van back at the hospital." He smiled, he seemed pleased with himself and rightly. I continued, "I honestly didn't think you were going to make it. I couldn't look." He thanked me, he was happy, it felt absolutely right to take the time to send a few words of appreciation in his direction before I disappeared, so I was glad I did.

*

I have trained myself to speak to people with love from my heart with a sincere desire for their joy and happiness. I wanted my life to be different, to feel different. To quote the great Michael Jackson, *"If you want to make the world a better place, take a look at yourself and make a change"*. I have spoken to the (wo)man in the mirror and I think I am doing okay. Well for the most part, I am only human after all and my chain can be yanked just like anyone else's. The major difference now is that it happens so rarely that the sensation is recognisable but unfamiliar. On these now rare occasions, I become instantly aware. I have a bag of tools and techniques at my disposal which I can reliably depend upon to return me easily and effortlessly to my preferred place of loving myself and loving others.

Hey, I may have said this before but there is no harm in running it by you again, that the search for knowledge of *Law of Attraction* often begins with wanting to find the home, the car, the money, the job or the partner. There is nothing wrong with that, I looked for some of those things too. I discovered that we can have all that and more.

What I also discovered was that all of these things and I mean all of these things, are secondary to the ultimate acquisition of a joyful, loving, peaceful heart. I am blessed, we all are and anyone can do what I have done. I have turned my life around in many ways and my anecdotes of how people respond to me are simply a glimpse of possibilities. I am glad I did the work. I am glad that I continue working towards feeling unconditional love for myself and others, which includes appreciating myself and appreciating others.

In my search for knowledge I had questions. I searched for answers. Suddenly I found something which made sense. It made absolute sense to me. My questions were answered. I discovered *'Ask And It Is Given'* lovingly brought to us by Esther and Jerry Hicks and this amazing book shares *The Teachings of Abraham,* explaining how universal law works for everyone, at all times, on all subjects, without exception. How cool is that? I had at last found something I could believe in, which did not contradict itself, something which gave and continues to give me absolute freedom. I feel excited for everyone I meet who is beginning to ask questions, who at least considers adding conscious deliberate 'creating' and 'attracting' to their life experience as they learn about the laws of the universe. I feel excited because it is exciting.

Knowledge and awareness of who I am now, gives me absolute power and freedom in each and every area of my life. It enables me to sleep well at night and wake up refreshed every morning with a keen and eager anticipation for the untold joy and wonder that lies ahead. Am I ever disappointed? No. How could I be disappointed when I have learned that my reaction to every situation is under my complete control? At the end of each day I have so very much to appreciate that I go to bed with my heart singing.

Phew, I had no intention of saying all that and I am not entirely sure where it all spewed from. Interestingly I was wondering how I would draw this publication to a close and finish my book. Well looking back at what I have just written with those few words about the joy of life, I feel that this is a suitable finale.

Thank you to my wonderful children, who continue to teach and inspire me every moment of every day. Bless you both.

Thank you to the Wholemeal Café angels, for creating a divine space and keeping me fed and watered during my many hours of writing. Bless you all.

Thank you to everyone I have ever met no matter how brief the interaction. Without all of you I would not be the person I am today and these books would not exist.

Just for fun, you will find information about my energy balancing treatments on www.massageforinnerpeace.co.uk where I have also have listed some of the books and music which have contributed to my journey. However top of my reading list is *'Ask And It Is Given – The Teachings of Abraham'*, Esther and Jerry Hicks as well as *'Illusions – The Adventures of a Reluctant Messiah'*, Richard Bach. Top of my listening list is anything by *Sacred Earth Music*, Prem and Joshua Williams.

If you fancy a little further browsing, you will find examples of my meditation inspired art on www.celestialcircles.co.uk

* * * * * *

A wise person once said, *'When we change the way we look at things, the things we look at change.'*

I wish for you everything I wish for myself, joy, love and peace

Carole